Word for Word

Word

for

WORD

James E. Snyder Jr.

A PERIGEE BOOK

A PERIGEE BOOK
Published by the Penguin Group
Penguin Group (USA) Inc.
375 Hudson Street, New York, New York 10014, USA

Penguin Group (Canada), 90 Eglinton Avenue East, Suite 700, Toronto, Ontario M4P 2Y3,
Canada (a division of Pearson Penguin Canada Inc.) • Penguin Books Ltd., 80 Strand,
London WC2R 0RL, England • Penguin Group Ireland, 25 St. Stephen's Green,
Dublin 2, Ireland (a division of Penguin Books Ltd.) • Penguin Group (Australia),
250 Camberwell Road, Camberwell, Victoria 3124, Australia (a division of Pearson
Australia Group Pty. Ltd.) • Penguin Books India Pvt. Ltd., 11 Community Centre,
Panchsheel Park, New Delhi—110 017, India • Penguin Group (NZ), 67 Apollo Drive,
Rosedale, North Shore 0632, New Zealand (a division of Pearson New Zealand Ltd.) •
Penguin Books (South Africa) (Pty.) Ltd., 24 Sturdee Avenue, Rosebank,
Johannesburg 2196, South Africa

Penguin Books Ltd., Registered Offices: 80 Strand, London WC2R 0RL, England

While the author has made every effort to provide accurate telephone numbers and
Internet addresses at the time of publication, neither the publisher nor the author assumes
any responsibility for errors, or for changes that occur after publication. Further, the
publisher does not have any control over and does not assume any responsibility for
author or third-party websites or their content.

First Perigee edition: December 2009
Adapted from *Lexical Semantics* by James E. Snyder Jr., published by Brown Walker Press
in 2007.

Library of Congress Cataloging-in-Publication Data

Snyder, James E. (James Eugene), 1945–
    Word for word / James E. Snyder Jr.
        p.   cm.
    ISBN 978-0-399-53538-3
    1. English language—Synonyms and antonyms.   I. Title.
    PE1591.S69   2009
    423'.12—dc22   2009029158

PRINTED IN THE UNITED STATES OF AMERICA

10   9   8   7   6   5   4   3   2   1

Most Perigee books are available at special quantity discounts for bulk purchases for sales
promotions, premiums, fund-raising, or educational use. Special books, or book excerpts,
can also be created to fit specific needs. For details, write: Special Markets, Penguin Group
(USA) Inc., 375 Hudson Street, New York, New York 10014.

To my sister

Jean Olive

A graceful lady who most

taught me to aspire

ACKNOWLEDGMENTS

I am eternally indebted to the many teachers, instructors, and professors under whom I have been fortunate to study. These include, among others, Coaches James Mashburn, Frank King, Vernon Price, Bob Callicutt, and Press Mull through secondary school; Coaches Bones McKinney, Dean Smith, Jack Murdock, Jim Layton, and Jack McClosky through university years; and Coaches Richard Jones and Mike Gurley.

The last thing my family wanted me to do was write another book. Once more they, and now even my grandchildren, from whose attention these projects take me, have been understanding.

My faithful staff, including Iris Hyatt, Chasity Clodfelter, Jennifer Wagoner, and Elizabeth Lancaster, have once more proved invaluable as I completed this project. I would like to express particular gratitude to four of my assistants to whom this book was primarily assigned. Cindy Venable, Erin Younts, Kristina Homesley, and Abby Younts have worked tirelessly and with remarkable precision in transcribing, proofing, and assisting me in coordinating the final draft.

Editing is always the final component for a written project. Nell Haynes Sharpe, my dedicated former English instructor, painstakingly reviewed each page of *Word for Word*. I am grateful for her guidance.

A high five goes to Marian Lizzi, editor in chief of Perigee Books. This manuscript caught her eye. She recognized my dream to create a simple way to collect and define many of the most extraordinary—and extraordinarily useful—words of our language, so that readers will never be at a loss for just the right word.

JES

CONTENTS

PART II

common words to
COMPLEX WORDS

PREFACE

One day a friend visited my law office and used the word *animadversion*. I was impressed. I didn't know what it meant. When our visit ended, I looked up the word in a dictionary. It was defined as *aspersion*—handy, if you know what *that* means. I soon learned that *aspersion* is defined as *calumny*. *Calumny?* I looked that one up, too, and discovered it means *slander*. Finally, a word I recognized.

This little exercise provided a valuable insight. If you don't know what a word means, the dictionary isn't always a useful resource. (To a lesser extent, the same is true if you don't know how to spell a word.)

One thing led to another, and before I knew it, I had a growing collection of lexicographic discoveries—the most beautiful, unusual, and nuanced words of our language, paired with their simpler, more familiar equivalents. This list proved to be surprisingly useful: Simpler than a dictionary and more straightforward than a thesaurus, it served as a handy desk reference—an at-a-glance guide to the words of Shakespeare, Wordsworth, and Longfellow, and many other writers and speakers of eras gone by.

In these days of emails, text messages, and frenetic multitasking, the beauty of our language is often lost. We tend to view words as a means to an end rather than a gloriously varied and appealing set of paints with which to express ourselves. We take precious little delight in selecting the right word for any given context or occasion. Sadly, something essential to our culture and our sense of selves has been lost.

Thus, *Word for Word* was created as a small gesture toward dialing back our modern sensibilities and making use of the wide array of spectacular words too many of us have forgotten or never known.

In my attempt to make this book as useful as possible, I have had to make a number of difficult choices. After all, not every complex word has a simple one-word definition. When there was a judgment call to make, I have opted for the most common, simple, generic, and encompassing word possible.

For the most part, "terms of art"—such as scientific, medical, and legal terms, and words specific to other realms—have been omitted. Words in this category are included if they are reasonably applicable in daily life.

I challenge the reader to learn every entry. This can be accomplished in a year by memorizing six words daily. But, as you know, it is easy to forget those words, so you must have a system. Each day you must not only learn six words but also review a number of words that you have previously learned. This process requires only a few minutes each day. Even a simple mind like mine or a great mind like yours can commit these words to memory and use them on a regular basis.

Part I, "COMPLEX WORDS to common words," invites the reader to absorb and enjoy the richness of alphabetized complex words. Part II, "common words to COMPLEX WORDS," provides unique access, via one-word definitions, to beautifully complex words you might never have used (or even come across) before.

Enjoy!

Word for Word

COMPLEX WORDS
to
common
words

A

ABDITIVE	hidden
ABDOMINOUS	overweight
ABECEDARIAN	beginner
ABIRRITANT	soothing
ABJECT	depressed
ABJURE	renounce
ABLACTATION	weaning
ABLATE	remove
ABLEPSIA	blindness
ABLUTION	washing
ABNEGATION	denial
ABRADE	criticize
ABREACTION	catharsis
ABSCISSION	removal
ABSQUATULATE	escape
ABSTEMIOUS	moderate
ABSTRACT	apart
ABSTRUSE	confusing
ACCELERANDO	quickening
ACCOUCHEMENT	birthing
ACCOUTRE	clothe
ACCOUTREMENT	accessory

ACCRESCENT	enlarging
ACERBIC	unruly
ACEROSE	needlelike
ACESCENT	souring
ACETOUS	sour
ACICULAR	needlelike
ACIDULOUS	biting
ACRASIA	excess
ACRID	bitter
ACRIMONY	harshness
ACROMEGALY	giant
ACULEATE	pointed
ACULEUS	sting
ADAMANTINE	firm
ADIPOSITY	obesity
ADJURE	swear
ADJUVANT	contributory
ADNEXA	appendages
ADSCITITIOUS	additional
ADULATORY	flattering
ADULTERATE	contaminate
ADUMBRATE	foreshadow
ADUST	burned
ADVENTITIOUS	accidental
ADVOLUTION	rolling
ADYNAMIC	weak
AEGIS	sponsorship
AERATE	ventilate
AERUGINOUS	blue
AFEBRILE	feverless
AFFLATUS	inspiration

AFFRIGHTED	afraid
AFFUSION	pouring
AGENESIA	nondevelopment
AGGERATE	heap
AGRESTIC	rustic
ALACRITY	eagerness
ALBESCENT	white
ALBICATION	whitening
ALEATORY	random
ALEXIA	illiteracy
ALGIDITY	coldness
ALIMENT	food
ALIMENTARY	nourishing
ALIQUOT	fractional
ALLEGORICAL	figurative
ALLIACEOUS	oniony
ALVEOLUS	cavity
AMALGAMATION	merging
AMANUENSIS	transcription
AMATIVE	amorous
AMATORY	sexual
AMBAGE	indirect
AMBIENT	surrounding
AMBUSCADE	ambush
AMELIORATE	improve
AMENITY	pleasantness
AMERCEMENT	penalty
AMORETTO	cupid
AMORPHOUS	shapeless
AMPHIGORY	unclear
AMULET	charm

ANABASIS	advance
ANABATIC	rising
ANACHRONISTIC	unchronological
ANAGOGIC	mystical
ANALITY	meticulousness
ANALOG	analogous
ANALOGUE	sameness
ANAMNESIS	remembering
ANAMORPHOSIS	distortion
ANASTATIC	risen
ANASTOMOSIS	union
ANATHEMA	curse
ANATOMIZE	analyze
ANCHORITE	hermit
ANCILLA	accessory
ANCIPITAL	double-edged
ANFRACTUOUS	winding
ANHELATION	hyperventilation
ANILE	senile
ANIMADVERSION	slander
ANIMUS	spirit
ANNALIST	historian
ANNECTENT	connecting
ANNULAR	ring-shaped
ANODYNE	anesthetic
ANOMALOUS	abnormal
ANOMALY	irregularity
ANSERINE	unwise
ANTEDILUVIAN	ancient
ANTHOLOGY	assortment
ANTHROPOMORPHIC	humanistic

ANTHROPOPHAGY	cannibalism
ANTIPATHY	dislike
ANTIPHONAL	hymnal
ANTIPHRASTIC	ironic
ANTIQUARIAN	collector
ANTITHESIS	opposite
ANUROUS	tailless
APERCUS	insight
APERIENT	laxative
APERTURE	opening
APHASIA	incomprehension
APHORISM	adage
APHOTIC	dark
APHRODISIAC	sexual
APICULATE	pointed
APOCATASTASIS	restoration
APOCRYPHAL	false
APODICTIC	irrefutable
APOGEE	culmination
APOGRAPH	copy
APOLAUSTIC	indulgent
APOLOGUE	allegory
APOSTASY	disloyalty
APOTHEGM	saying
APOTHEOSIS	ideal
APPANAGE	endowment
APPELLATION	name
APPETENCE	craving
APPOSITE	pertinent
APPURTENANCE	accessory
APPURTENANT	accompanying

AQUILINE	curved
AQUIVER	agitated
ARBOREOUS	wooded
ARCANE	mysterious
ARCHETYPE	original
ARENOSE	sandy
ARGENT	silver
ARGOSY	fleet
ARGOT	slang
ARRANT	complete
ARROGATE	seize
ARTIFICE	trick
ASCETIC	abstinent
ASCRIPTION	attribution
ASEPTIC	germless
ASEXUALIZATION	sterilization
ASKANCE	distrustfully
ASONANT	soundless
ASPERITY	roughness
ASPERSION	slander
ASSEVERATE	proclaim
ASSIDUOUS	diligent
ASSIGNATION	appointment
ASSUAGE	satisfy
ASSURGENT	rising
ASTHENIC	weak
ASTRINGENT	constrictive
ASYMPTOTE	tangent
ATARACTIC	calming
ATAVISM	throwback
ATELIER	studio

ATHANASIA	immortality
ATHWART	across
ATRABILIOUS	gloomy
ATTENUATE	weaken
AUBERGINE	eggplant
AUDACIOUS	bold
AUGMENT	enlarge
AUGURY	prophecy
AULIC	courtly
AUSCULTATION	listening
AUSTERE	stern
AUTARKY	independence
AUTOCHTHONOUS	native
AUTOCLAVE	sterilize
AUTODIDACTIC	self-taught
AUTOEROTISM	self-arousal
AUTOGENOUSLY	independently
AUTOMATON	robot
AVARICIOUS	greedy
AVATAR	embodiment
AVERRUNCATE	avert
AVIDITY	eagerness
AVOLATE	escape
AVULSION	tearing
AVUNCULAR	uncle-like
AWRY	deviating
AXIOMATIC	true

B

BACCHANALIAN	drunken
BACILLUS	bacterium
BACULINE	rodlike
BADINAGE	teasing
BAGATELLE	trifle
BAGNIO	cathouse
BALBUTIATE	stammer
BALEFUL	harmful
BANAL	ordinary
BANAUSIC	practical
BANDOLIER	belt
BAROQUE	ornate
BARRATRY	litigiousness
BASTINADO	beating
BATEAUX	boats
BATHOS	sentimentality
BEATIFIC	blissful
BEDIZEN	gaudy
BELAY	stop
BEMUSE	confuse
BENIGNANT	kind

BENISON	blessing
BERCEUSE	lullaby
BESEEM	suitable
BESOM	broom
BESPANGLE	sprinkle
BIBLIOPHILE	book collector
BIBLIOPOLE	bookseller
BIBULOUS	absorbent
BIFURCATE	divide
BILLINGSGATE	vulgarity
BINATE	paired
BISQUE	soup
BLITHE	merry
BOEOTIAN	stupid person
BOISERIE	paneling
BOMBINATE	hum
BOOBOISIE	uneducated
BORBORYGMUS	flatulent
BOSCAGE	thicket
BOURGEOIS	middle-class
BOWDLERIZE	cleanse
BRACHYLOGY	conciseness
BRAIDISM	hypnotism
BRASQUE	clay
BREASTWORK	fortification
BRETESSE	battlement
BREVETTED	ranked
BRIGANTINE	sailboat
BROBDINGNAGIAN	huge
BUCCAL	cheek

BUCENTAUR	barge
BUCOLIC	rustic
BUMPTIOUS	self-assertive
BUSKY	wooded
BYSSACEOUS	linen-like

C

CABAL	group
CABOODLE	lot
CACHE	storage
CACHET	seal
CACHEXIA	ill health
CACHINNATE	laugh
CACODEMON	evil spirit
CACOPHONY	harshness
CADAVEROUS	ghastly
CADGE	borrow
CADUCOUS	brief
CAIRD	vagrant
CAIRN	memorial
CALABASH	gourd
CALDERA	crater
CALEFACIENT	heating
CALIGINOUS	dark
CALPAC	hat
CALUMET	pipe
CALUMNY	slander
CAMBRIC	linen
CAMPESTRAL	rural

CANARD	lie
CANESCENT	grayish
CANNULAR	tubular
CANONICAL	conforming
CANOROUS	melodic
CANT	tilt
CANTON	division
CANTONMENT	quarters
CAPACIOUS	roomy
CAPIAS	warrant
CAPILLAMENT	thread
CAPONIZE	alter
CAPRICIOUS	impulsive
CAPTIOUS	fault-finding
CARCINOMA	cancer
CARIOUS	rotten
CARNIVOROUS	meat-eating
CARPING	complaining
CARTOGRAPHER	mapper
CASEOUS	cheesy
CASHIER	dismiss
CASTELLATED	turreted
CASTIGATE	criticize
CASUISTIC	rational
CASUISTRY	deceptiveness
CATENATE	link
CAVEAT	warning
CAVIL	quibble
CELERITY	speediness
CEMENTITIOUS	hard
CENSORIOUS	critical

CENTRIPETAL	inward
CERAS	horn
CERULEAN	blue
CERUMEN	earwax
CHAMPERTOUS	joining
CHAMPIGNON	mushroom
CHAPARRAL	thicket
CHARINESS	caution
CHARY	cautious
CHAUVINISM	unreasonableness
CHEVRON	V-shaped
CHILBLAINED	swollen
CHIMERA	illusion
CHIMERICAL	imaginary
CHIROGRAPHY	penmanship
CHOLERIC	irritable
CHOPLOGIC	disputing
CHTHONIC	ghostly
CHUFFINESS	surliness
CHURLISH	boorish
CICATRIZED	healed
CICERONE	guide
CINCTURE	belt
CIRCUMFERENTIAL	circle-like
CIRCUMFLUENT	flowing
CIRCUMJACENT	surrounding
CIRCUMLOCUTION	wordiness
CIRCUMSCRIBED	zoned
CIRCUMSCRIPTION	definition
CIRCUMVOLUTION	revolution
CLARY	flavoring

CLAUDICATION	limping
CLERESTORY	gallery
CLIMACTERIC	crucial
CLOCHARD	vagrant
CLOCHER	bell tower
CLOISTRESS	nun
CLOTURE	end
COADJUTOR	assistant
COAPTATION	fastening
COCKADE	knot
CODICIL	supplement
COEFFICIENT	number
COEVAL	contemporaneous
COGENT	convincing
COGNATE	kin
COGNOMEN	surname
COGNOSCENTE	expert
COLLEGIALITY	cooperation
COLLET	collar
COLLOCATE	gather
COLORABLE	believable
COLUMBARIUM	niches
COMEDO	blackhead
COMESTIBLE	edible
COMITY	courteousness
COMMINATION	vengeance
COMMODIOUS	roomy
COMPENDIUM	summary
COMPLAISANT	agreeable
COMPORTMENT	behavior
COMPUNCTION	remorse

CONCATENATION	integration
CONCERTATION	assistance
CONCINNITY	harmony
CONCINNOUS	well-dressed
CONCOMITANT	accompanying
CONCUPISCENCE	sexuality
CONCUPISCENT	sexual
CONDIGN	merited
CONDOTTIERE	mercenary
CONEPATE	skunk
CONFABULATE	chat
CONFLATION	blending
CONFUTATION	disputation
CONGEABLE	legal
CONGERIES	piles
CONIFER	evergreen
CONJURE	adjure
CONNUBIAL	marital
CONODONT	fossil
CONSANGUINITY	blood relation
CONSENTANEOUS	agreeing
CONSERVATORY	greenhouse
CONSIMILITUDE	resemblance
CONSONANCE	accord
CONSPECTUS	outline
CONSTUPRATE	rape
CONSUBSTANTIATE	proclaim
CONSUETUDINARY	customary
CONTERMINOUS	contiguous
CONTESTATION	dispute
CONTINENCE	chastity

CONTRETEMPS	embarrassment
CONTRISTATION	dejection
CONTUMACIOUS	disobedient
CONTUMELIOUS	embarrassing
CONUNDRUM	riddle
CONURBATION	urbanization
CONVENTICLE	meeting
CONVIVIAL	friendly
COOPTION	election
COPROLALIA	obscenity
COQUETTISH	flirtatious
CORPOSANT	fireball
CORPULENT	fat
CORRIGENDUM	error
CORSAIR	pirate
CORTINA	curtain
CORUSCATE	sparkle
CORUSCATION	brightness
CORYBANTIC	frenzied
COSTIVENESS	closeness
COSTREL	flask
COTERIE	group
COUCHANT	prone
COUNTERMINOUS	adjoining
COUNTERVAIL	compensate
COURTESAN	prostitute
COZEN	cheat
CRAPULENCE	gluttony
CRAPULOUS	gluttonous
CRASSITUDE	dumbness
CRAVEN	cowardly

CREPITATION	crackling
CREPUSCULAR	dim
CREPUSCULE	evening
CRIBRIFORM	perforated
CROTCHET	whim
CRYPTIC	puzzling
CUDGEL	club
CUMSHAW	gratuity
CUNCTATION	postponement
CUNCTATIVE	procrastinating
CUNCTIPOTENT	all-powerful
CUPIDINOUS	greedy
CUPIDITY	greed
CUSHAT	pigeon
CUSTUMAL	law book
CYCLOPEAN	huge
CYNOSURE	hub

D

DACTYL	finger
DAEDAL	skillful
DANDLE	dance
DEALBATION	bleaching
DEASIL	clockwise
DEBELLATION	conquering
DECAMP	move
DECENNIUM	decade
DECIDUOUS	hardwood
DECLIVITY	downward
DÉCOLLETAGE	neckline
DECRESCENT	ending
DECUSSATE	crossing
DEDIFFERENTIATION	change
DEESIS	prayer
DEFALCATION	embezzlement
DEFENESTRATE	throw out
DEFERVESCENCE	cooling
DEFILADE	fortification
DEFLAGRATE	burn
DEFLORATION	ravishing
DEGLUTITION	swallowing

DEHISCENT	opening
DEICTIC	proven
DEIGNOUS	arrogant
DEIPNOSOPHIST	communicant
DELASSATION	exhaustion
DELECTATION	pleasure
DELIQUESCE	melt
DELUSIVE	deceptive
DEMERGE	immerse
DEMIGOD	god-man
DEMILUNE	crescent
DEMIMONDE	prostitutes
DEMULCENT	soothing
DENDROPHILOUS	treelike
DENIGRATOR	defamer
DENOUEMENT	revelation
DENUDE	strip
DEONTOLOGY	morality
DERACINATE	uproot
DESICCATE	dried
DESIDERATE	wishful
DESPONSATE	betroth
DESUETUDE	disuse
DESULTORY	random
DETERGE	wash
DETRITUS	piece
DETUMESCENCE	reduction
DETURBATE	evict
DEUTEROPATHY	unusualness
DEVOLUTION	degeneration
DEXTRAL	right-handed

DIADEM	headband
DIALAGE	change
DIALECTIC	logical
DIAPHANOUS	transparent
DIATRIBE	criticism
DICHOTOMY	division
DIDACTIC	teaching
DIFFIDENT	reserved
DILATANT	expanding
DILETTANTE	superficial
DIMINUTIVE	tiny
DIPSOMANIAC	alcoholic
DISABUSED	errorless
DISAPPROBATION	disapproval
DISCALCED	shoeless
DISCERP	rip
DISCERPTIBLE	partitionable
DISCOMFITURE	embarrassment
DISCRETE	separate
DISCURSIVE	rambling
DISESTABLISH	terminate
DISESTABLISHED	xed
DISESTABLISHMENT	deprivation
DISESTABLISHMENTARIAN	depriver
DISGORGE	unload
DISHABILLE	disarray
DISINGENUOUS	insincere
DISPARATE	distinct
DISPITEOUS	cruel
DISPUTATION	debate
DISQUISITION	discussion

DISSIDENCE	dissent
DISSILIENT	erupting
DISSONANCE	discord
DISTRAIT	forgetful
DITHYRAMBIC	excited
DIURNAL	daily
DIVA	goddess
DIVAGATE	wander
DIVAGATION	digression
DOGGEREL	trivial
DOLMEN	prehistoric
DOLOROUS	mournful
DOLTISH	stupid
DOTATION	endowment
DOUR	stern
DOWSABEL	sweetheart
DOYEN	senior
DRAFFISH	worthless
DRAMATURGIC	theatrical
DRECK	inferior
DRIEGH	dreary
DRIVEL	nonsense
DROSS	waste
DUBIOSITY	uncertainty
DUDGEON	resentment
DUENNA	chaperone
DULCETLY	melodiously
DYSPEPSIA	indigestion
DYSPHORIA	nervousness

E

EBULLITION	bubbling
ECCHYMOSIS	bruise
ECCLESIA	audience
ECHELONS	levels
ECHOPRAXIA	mimicking
ECLECTIC	mixed
ECTETHMOID	sieve
ECTOMORPHIC	slender
EDACIOUS	gluttonous
EDUCE	procure
EFFLEURAGE	rubbing
EFFLICACIOUS	effective
EFFLORESCENCE	fulfillment
EFFLUENCE	outflow
EFFLUVIUM	emanation
EFFRONTERY	nerve
EFFULGENCE	brilliance
EFFULGENT	beaming
EGALITARIAN	equal
EGREGIOUS	horrible
EIDOLON	imaginary
ÉLAN	spirit

ELDRITCH	weird
ELEEMOSYNARY	charitable
ELEGICAL	mournful
ELEGY	poem
ELENCHUS	dispute
ELEPHANTIASIS	enlargement
ELINGUID	tongue-tied
ELOCUTION	speaking
ELYSIAN	blissful
EMASCULATE	weaken
EMBOUCHURE	mouth
EMEND	edit
EMETIC	vomit-inducing
EMOLLIENT	relaxing
EMOLUMENT	salary
EMPIRICAL	verifiable
EMPTION	buying
EMPYREAN	heaven
EMULSIVE	yielding
ENCINCTURE	surround
ENCOMIUM	praise
ENCUMBRANCE	burden
ENDEMIC	localized
ENDENIZATION	naturalization
ENDOGENOUS	independently
ENIGMA	confusion
ENIGMATOGRAPHY	riddle
ENISLE	isolate
ENNUI	boredom
ENSCONCED	sheltered
ENSEMBLE	performers

ENSORCEL	bewitch
ENTELECHY	awakening
ENTOIL	trap
ENTROPY	disorder
EPHEMERAL	short-lived
EPICENE	effeminate
EPIGONE	follower
EPIGRAM	saying
EPIGRAMMATIC	concise
EPIPHANY	awakening
EPISTOLARY	letters
EPITHALAMIUM	ode
EPITHET	disparagement
EPITHYMETIC	passionate
EQUABLE	steady
EQUICEDE	dirge
EQUIPAGE	equipment
EQUIPOLLENT	equivalent
EQUIPONDERANT	balanced
EQUIVOQUE	pun
EREMITE	hermit
ERETHISM	stimulation
ERISTIC	argumentative
EROGENOUS	arousing
ERSATZ	artificial
ERUCT	belch
ERUCTATE	burp
ERUDITION	scholarship
ERUMPENT	thrusting
ESCALADE	scale
ESCARPMENT	cliff

ESCHATOLOGY	afterlife
ESCHEAT	confiscate
ESCRITOIRE	desk
ESCULENT	edible
ESCUTCHEON	shield
ESOTERIC	confidential
ESPLANADE	plain
ESTABLISHMENTARIAN	orthodox
ESURIENT	greedy
ETATISM	socialism
ETERNE	everlasting
ETESIAN	yearly
ETHEREAL	airy
ETHNOCENTRICITY	racism
ETIOLATE	whiten
ETIOLOGY	cause
EUDEMONIA	happiness
EUPHUISTIC	eloquent
EUTECTIC	thawing
EVAGATION	wandering
EVANESCE	vanish
EVISCERATE	deprive
EXARATE	plow
EXCELSIOR	shavings
EXCLAMATION	explanation
EXCORIATE	criticize
EXCREMENT	feces
EXCRESCENCE	wart
EXCULPATE	acquit
EXCURSIVE	meandering
EXECRATED	detested

EXECRATIVE	detestable
EXEGESIS	explanation
EXEGETICAL	explanatory
EXHORTATORY	encouraging
EXIGENCY	urgency
EXIGUOUS	meager
EXIMIOUS	excellent
EXISTENTIAL	veritable
EXORDIUM	beginning
EXPATIATING	talkative
EXPIATE	atone
EXPONENT	symbol
EXPOSE	reveal
EXPOSTULATE	object
EXPOSTULATION	objection
EXPURGATE	edit
EXSUCCOUS	dry
EXTIRPATE	destroy
EXTIRPATION	removal
EXTRAPOLATE	speculate
EXTRAVASATE	flow

F

FACETIOUS	flippant
FACILE	accomplishable
FACINOROUS	wicked
FACTITIOUS	artificial
FACTOTUM	servant
FACULTATIVE	authoritative
FAINÉANT	lazy
FANFARON	braggart
FANION	flag
FARCEUR	joker
FARDEL	encumbrance
FARINACEOUS	starchy
FASCINE	brushwood
FASTNESS	stronghold
FATIDIC	prophetic
FATUOUS	foolish
FAUTEUIL	armchair
FEALTY	fidelity
FECKLESS	worthless
FECULENT	foul
FECUND	fertile
FECUNDITY	fertility

FELICITOUS	pleasant
FEMME FATALE	seductress
FENESTRATED	pierced
FERAL	natural
FERITY	wildness
FERRIAGE	fare
FERULE	discipline
FERVID	zealous
FESTINATE	hastening
FETED	praised
FETID	stinking
FIDDLE-FADDLE	trifle
FILCH	steal
FILIBUSTER	invade
FILIGREE	openwork
FISTULA	passage
FIVER	money
FLACCID	limp
FLAGELLATE	whip
FLAGITIOUS	wicked
FLAMBEAU	flame
FLECHE	steeple
FLEER	laugh
FLIVVER	car
FLORID	flowery
FLUMMERY	flattery
FLUMMOXED	confused
FLURRIED	agitated
FOMENTER	troublemaker
FORFEND	avert
FORSWEAR	renounce

FRACTIOUS	quarrelsome
FRANGIBLE	fragile
FRENETIC	frantic
FRISSON	thrill
FROIDEUR	aloofness
FROUFROU	swishing
FROWSTY	musty
FUGACIOUS	fleeting
FULGURATION	flash
FULIGINOUS	hidden
FULMINATE	denounce
FULSOME	disgusting
FUMAROLE	vent
FUNDAMENT	buttocks
FUNEREAL	mournful
FUNGIBLE	indistinguishable
FURCIFEROUS	disgusting
FURTIVELY	stealthily
FUSCOUS	lightless
FUSILLADE	gunfire
FUSTIAN	exaggeration
FUSTIGATE	punish

G

GAINSAY	deny
GALIMATIAS	confusion
GALLIVANT	wander
GALVANIC	electric
GAMASHES	boots
GARRULITY	talkativeness
GARRULOUS	talkative
GASCONADING	boasting
GAUCHE	tactless
GELID	chilly
GENICULATION	knottiness
GENRE	category
GENUFLECT	bend
GEODESIC	straight
GEOPONIC	agrarian
GIBBOUS	swelling
GLABROUS	smooth
GLISSADE	glide
GLISTER	luster
GLOAMING	twilight
GLOBOSE	spherical
GLOPPEN	frighten

GLOSSOLALIA	unintelligibility
GNATHONIC	flattering
GNEISS	granite
GNOSIS	mystical
GOMEREL	fool
GONIMIUM	productive
GORMLESS	stupid
GOURMAND	glutton
GRACILE	thin
GRAMARYE	magic
GRAMINEOUS	grassy
GRANDILOQUENT	bombastic
GRATULANCE	bribe
GRAVAMEN	essential
GREGARIOUS	friendly
GRENADINE	reddish
GRIFTER	swindler
GROUSING	nagging
GULOSITOUS	gluttonous
GYROSE	wavy

H

HABILIMENT	clothing
HALATION	blurring
HALCYON	calm
HARIOLATION	prognostication
HARLEQUIN	comic
HAUTEUR	haughtiness
HAVEREL	fool
HEBDOMEDAL	weekly
HEBETUDE	dullness
HECTOR	swagger
HEDONISTIC	pleasurable
HEGEMONY	authority
HEGIRA	exodus
HEINIE	buttocks
HELICAL	spiral
HELIOCENTRIC	sun-centered
HELIOSIS	sunstroke
HELIOTROPE	purplish
HEPTACOLIC	limb
HEREDITAMENT	inheritance
HERMETIC	magical
HETAERA	prostitute

HETEROCHTHONOUS	foreign
HETERODOX	unorthodox
HETEROGENEOUS	mixed
HEURISTIC	teaching
HIERATIC	priestly
HIRCINE	lustful
HIRSUTE	hairy
HISTOGENESIS	growth
HISTRIONIC	theatrical
HOLOGRAPHIC	handwritten
HOMERIC	heroic
HOMILY	sermon
HOMOEROTICISM	homosexuality
HOMOGAMY	inbreeding
HOMOLOGATE	approve
HOMOLOGATION	confirmation
HOMUNCULUS	midget
HONESTATION	adornment
HOROLOGE	clock
HORTATIVE	encouraging
HOUYHNHNM	horse
HOYDEN	tomboy
HUBRIS	pride
HUMECTANT	wetness
HUMORSOMELY	oddly
HUNTCOUNTER	hound
HUSBANDMAN	farmer
HYALOD	transparent
HYDROPHILIC	soluble
HYDROPHOBIC	insoluble
HYPERBOLE	exaggeration

HYPERBOREAN	frigid
HYPEREMESIS	vomiting
HYPNAGOGIC	sleepy
HYPNOPEDIA	education
HYPOSTASAS	trinity
HYPOSTATIZE	externalize
HYPOTHECATE	pledge
HYPOTHESIS	theory
HYPOXEMIA	suffocation

I

IATROGENIC	disease-causing
ICHNEYMON	tracker
ICON	saint
ICONOCLAST	destroyer
ICONOSTASIS	screen
IDENTIC	same
IDEOGRAM	symbol
IDIOM	dialect
IDIOPATHIC	uncertain
IDIOSYNCRACY	peculiarity
IDONEOUS	suitable
IGNEOUS	volcanic
ILLAQUEATION	ensnaring
ILLATION	inference
ILLECEBROUS	attractive
ILLIBERAL	uncultured
ILLIQUID	cashless
IMBROGLIO	entanglement
IMMATERIATE	immaterial
IMMEDICABLE	incurable
IMMISCIBLE	unmixable
IMMOLATE	sacrifice

IMMURED	imprisoned
IMMUTABLE	unchangeable
IMPEDIMENTA	suitcase
IMPERCIPIENT	misunderstood
IMPERIOUS	lordly
IMPERTURBATION	unflappability
IMPIETY	idolatry
IMPOLITIC	rash
IMPONE	wager
IMPOROUS	dense
IMPORTUNATE	solicit
IMPORTUNE	beg
IMPORTUOUS	harborless
IMPOSTUMATE	gather
IMPRECATION	curse
IMPRESARIO	conductor
IMPREST	loan
IMPROVIDENT	unprepared
IMPUDENCE	disregard
IMPUGNED	admonished
IMPUISSANCE	feeble
IMPUTRESCIBLE	moral
INACQUIESCENT	refusing
INALIENABLE	unsalable
INAMORATA	lover
INANE	empty
INANITION	exhaustion
INCANTATION	chanting
INCHOATE	incomplete
INCIPIENT	awakening
INCISIVE	direct

INCIVISM	antigovernment
INCOMMODIOUS	inconvenient
INCONSONANT	inconsistent
INCONY	pretty
INCORPOREAL	formless
INCUBUS	nightmare
INCULPATE	blame
INCUNABULA	beginnings
INDAGATE	search
INDEFATIGABLE	tireless
INDIFFERENT	unbiased
INDIGENOUS	native
INDISCERPTIBLE	inseparable
INDOLENT	lazy
INDULGENCE	fulfillment
INDURATE	callous
INDURATED	hardened
INEFFABLE	unspeakable
INELUCTABLE	irresistible
INENARRABLE	indescribable
INERT	powerless
INEXORABLE	relentless
INFIDEL	unbeliever
INGANNATION	deceit
INGEMINATE	repeat
INGLORIOUS	shameful
INGRAVESCENT	worsening
INGUINAL	groin
INIMICAL	unfriendly
INIMITABLE	matchless
INIQUITOUS	wicked

INNOCUOUS	harmless
INOSCULATE	join
INSATIATE	insatiable
INSCRUTABLE	mysterious
INSENSATE	infatuate
INSIPID	tasteless
INSOLENT	rude
INSOUCIANT	lighthearted
INSPIRIT	encourage
INSPISSATED	thickened
INSUFFLATE	ventilate
INSULAR	local
INSURGENT	rebel
INTELLECTION	hold
INTEMPERANCE	drunkenness
INTERCALATE	insert
INTERCALATION	addition
INTERDICT	destroy
INTERLARDED	intersperse
INTERLOCUTION	conversation
INTERNECINE	kill
INTERNUNCIAL	proclaiming
INTERPOLATE	insert
INTERREGNUM	leaderless
INTERROGATORIES	questions
INTERSTICES	crevices
INTRACTABILITY	obstinateness
INTRANSIGENT	uncompromising
INTREPID	fearless
INTROMIT	confess
INTUITED	understanding

INTUMESCENT	charring
INTUSSUSCEPT	enclose
INVAGINATE	enclose
INVECTIVE	insulting
INVEIGLE	flatter
INVETERATE	habitual
INVIDIOUS	obnoxious
INVIGILATION	observation
IONIZED	charged
IRENIC	peaceful
IRREDENTISM	inclusion
IRREFRAGABLE	irrefutable
IRREMEDIABLE	unsolvable
ISOMORPHIC	identical
ITERATION	repetition
ITHYPALLIC	lustful

J

JACTATION	boasting
JACULATE	throw
JANISSARY	supportive
JECTIGATION	shaking
JEJUNE	unsatisfying
JINGOISM	nationalism
JITNEY	bus
JOCOSERIOUS	joke
JOCUND	happy
JUNTO	revolution
JUTE	fiber
JUVENESCENT	youthful
JUXTAPOSED	adjacent

K

KARYOGAMY	nuclei
KEMP	champion
KIBOSH	stop
KINESIS	motion
KINESTHETIC	muscular
KINETIC	active
KINGBOLT	kingpin
KNOUT	knife
KVETCH	complain
KWAIKEN	knife

L

LABEFACTION	revolution
LABEFY	weaken
LABILE	unstable
LABYRINTHIAN	winding
LACHES	delay
LACHRYMOSE	tearful
LACONIC	curt
LACRIMAL	crying
LAMBENT	bright
LANCEOLATE	tapering
LANCINATING	stabbing
LANGUET	tongue
LANGUOR	sluggishness
LANGUOROUS	listless
LANUGINOUS	hairy
LAPACTIC	purging
LARBOARD	left
LARGESSE	generosity
LASCIVIOUS	lustful
LASSITUDE	fatigue
LEGERDEMAIN	trickery
LEGERITY	alacrity

LEGGIADROUS	polished
LEITMOTIF	recurrence
LENITY	gentleness
LENTIGINOUS	spotted
LEONINE	fierce
LEUKOUS	white
LEVEE	reception
LEVIGATE	powderize
LEVIGATED	polished
LEXICON	dictionary
LIBIDINOUS	lustful
LICENTIOUSNESS	lewd
LIEGE	follower
LIGATION	bond
LILLIPUTIAN	small
LIMACINE	sluglike
LIMN	draw
LIMPID	clear
LINEAMENT	outline
LIONIZATION	enhancement
LISSOME	nimble
LISTENABLE	considering
LITOTES	understatement
LITTORAL	shore
LITURATE	spotted
LIVOR	malignity
LONGANIMITY	patience
LONGILATERAL	long-sided
LOQUACIOUS	talkative
LOQUENCE	eloquence
LOUCHE	shifty

LOUT	clumsy
LOUTISH	boorish
LUBRICIOUS	obscene
LUBRICITY	oily
LUCENT	bright
LUCERN	lamp
LUCUBRATION	study
LUGUBRIOUS	mournful
LUXATION	dislocation
LYSIS	disappearance

M

MACABRE	gruesome
MACERATE	soak
MACHINATION	plot
MACROBIOSIS	longevity
MACULATE	blemish
MAELSTROM	whirlpool
MAGNILOQUENT	bombastic
MAGNOLIACEOUS	magnolia-like
MAINSWORN	perjured
MALADROIT	awkward
MALAPERT	bold
MALAPROPISM	inappropriateness
MALEDICENT	slanderous
MALEDICTION	curse
MALEFACTOR	evildoer
MALEFIC	harmful
MALEFICIATE	bewitch
MALENTENDU	misunderstanding
MALEVOLENT	malicious
MALINGERER	faker
MALODOROUS	stinking
MANDAMUS	command

MANDARIN	official
MANÈGE	horsemanship
MANSUETUDE	gentleness
MANUDUCTION	instruction
MANUMISSION	emancipation
MANUMIT	free
MASOCHISM	self-deprivation
MASTERDOM	rule
MASTICATE	chew
MATINAL	morning
MATRIX	mold
MAUMET	idol
MAUNDER	wander
MAVIN	expert
MAWKISH	sentimental
MEGALOMANIA	arrogance
MEGRIM	impulse
MEIOSIS	understatement
MÉLANGE	mixture
MELLIFLUOUS	smoothly
MENDACIOUS	dishonest
MENDICANT	beggar
MEPHITIC	poisonous
MEPHITIS	stench
MERETRICIOUS	gaudy
MERITOCRATIC	deserved
METALLOID	nonmetal
METAPHYSICAL	philosophical
METASTASIZE	spread
METRONOMIC	regular
MIASMIC	poisonous

MICTURITION	urination
MILIEU	environment
MILLIARD	billion
MIMETIC	imitative
MISANDRIST	man-hater
MISANTHROPY	hatred
MISAVER	misspeak
MISCREANT	villain
MISPRISION	misunderstanding
MNEMONIC	memory aid
MODERNITY	contemporary
MOIETY	half
MOLIMINOUS	momentous
MOLLIFY	pacify
MONIKER	name
MONILIFORM	beaded
MONOGRAPHIC	single
MONTAGE	composite
MORDACIOUS	biting
MORDANCY	sarcasm
MORDANT	biting
MOREL	sponge
MORIBUND	dying
MORIGERATE	trustworthy
MORONIC	stupid
MOSCHATE	musky
MUCILAGIOUS	slimy
MUCK	manure
MULIEBRITY	womanhood
MULISH	stubborn
MULTIFARIOUSNESS	diverseness

MUNIFICENT	bountiful
MUNIMENT	defense
MUTABLE	changeable
MUTUATION	loaning
MYRMIDON	henchman
MYRRHED	fragranced
MYTHOMANIA	exaggeration

N

NARCISSISM	vanity
NARCOMANIA	addiction
NARCOSIS	unconsciousness
NARTHEX	vestibule
NASCENT	new
NATANT	floating
NAUFRAGE	shipwreck
NAUPATHIA	seasickness
NEBBISH	introvert
NECESSITOUS	urgent
NECROPOLIS	graveyard
NECROPSY	autopsy
NECROTIC	dead
NEFARIOUS	bad
NEOPLASM	tumor
NEOTERIC	new
NESCIENCE	ignorance
NEXUS	link
NICTITATE	blink
NIFFER	barter
NIHILISTIC	skeptical
NIMBUS	cloud

NIMIETY	redundancy
NIVEOUS	snowy
NOCTAMBULIST	sleepwalker
NOCTULE	bat
NOCUOUS	harmful
NODDY	fool
NOETIC	intellectual
NOMOTHETE	legislator
NONPAREIL	peerless
NONPLUSSED	perplexed
NORMATIVE	standard
NOSTOMANIA	homesickness
NUBILATE	cloud
NUBILE	attractive
NUDATION	stripping
NUGATORY	powerless
NUMINOUS	divine
NUMMULAR	coinlike
NUTATION	nod
NYCHTHEMERON	day and night
NYMPHOLEPSY	rapture

O

OBDURATE	inflexible
OBEISANCE	respect
OBFUSCATE	confuse
OBITER	incidentally
OBLATION	offering
OBLIQUITY	indirectness
OBLITERATIVE	indistinct
OBLIVESCENCE	forgetfulness
OBLOQUY	disgrace
OBMUTESCENT	mute
OBNUBILATE	darken
OBNUBILATION	confusion
OBREPTION	fraud
OBROGATION	annulment
OBSCURANTISM	confusion
OBSCURATION	darkening
OBSECRATE	plead
OBSEQUIOUS	slavish
OBSEQUY	funeral rite
OBSTIPATION	constipation
OBSTREPEROUSNESS	unruliness
OBSTRICTION	obligation

OBTRUDE	interrupt
OBTURATION	closing
OBTUSE	blunt
OBVIATE	prevent
OBVOLUTE	overlapping
OCCIDENTAL	western
OCHLOCRACY	mobocracy
OCHLOCRATIC	riotous
ODALISQUE	concubine
ODDMENT	fragment
ODIBLE	hateful
ODIUM	hatred
ODONTALGIA	toothache
OENOLOGY	wine study
OFFAL	waste
OLEAGINOUS	oily
OLEOPHILIC	oil receptive
OLEOPHOBIC	oil repellent
OLIBANUM	perfume
ONOMATOPOEIA	imitation
OPALESCENT	iridescent
OPAQUE	lightless
OPEROSE	laborious
OPEROSENESS	business
OPHIDIAN	snake
OPPROBRIUM	disgrace
OPPUGN	assail
OPPUGNANT	hostile
OPTATE	desire
ORACULAR	inspired
ORDURE	wasteful

ORECTIC	desiring
ORGULOUS	proud
ORIFICE	opening
ORISON	prayer
ORTIVE	eastern
OSCITANT	drowsy
OSCITATION	yawn
OSCULATION	kiss
OSMATIC	smelling
OSMOSIS	absorption
OSSEAN	bony
OSSIFY	harden
OTIOSE	idle
OTIOSITY	idleness
OXYMORON	incongruous
OZOSTOMIA	halitosis

P

PACHYDERMATOUS	thickened
PAEAN	praise
PAGINATE	number
PALABRA	word
PALAVER	chatter
PALINGENETIC	rebirth
PALISADE	stake
PALLIATE	conceal
PALLIATIVE	mitigative
PALUDISM	malaria
PANACEA	cure-all
PANDEMIC	diseased
PANEGYRIC	eulogy
PANJANDRUM	pretender
PANOPLY	covering
PANTAGRUELISM	temperament
PANTHEON	cathedral
PARACLETE	advocate
PARADIGM	pattern
PARAGON	model
PARALOGISM	falsehood
PARAPET	wall

PARCENARY	joint
PARENESIS	advice
PARESTHESIA	tingling
PARLOUS	dangerous
PARODY	imitation
PARONOMASIA	pun
PAROXYSM	fit
PARSIMONIOUS	frugal
PARTITION	division
PARTURITION	childbirth
PASQUINADE	satire
PATERFAMILIAS	father
PATHOGEN	bacterium
PATHOGENIC	diseased
PATHOS	pity
PATRICIATE	aristocracy
PATRIMONY	inheritance
PATRONYMIC	surname
PATULOUS	exposed
PECCABLE	mistaken
PECULATION	embezzlement
PEDAGOGY	teaching
PEDANTIC	showy
PEDERASTY	sodomy
PEDESTRIAN	commonplace
PEJORATIVE	disparaging
PELAGIC	oceanic
PELLUCID	transparent
PENURIOUS	stingy
PENURY	poor
PERADVENTURE	chance

PERCHANCE	perhaps
PERDITION	hell
PERDURE	last
PEREGRINATE	walk
PEREGRINATION	journey
PERFERVID	zealous
PERFIDY	faithlessness
PERFORCE	necessarily
PERIGEE	culmination
PERIPATETIC	itinerant
PERIPHRASIS	verbiage
PERIPHRASTIC	wordy
PERJURIOUS	lying
PERMANSION	continuance
PERMEABLE	porous
PERNICIOUS	destructive
PERORATION	conclusion
PERSIFLAGE	banter
PERSPICACIOUS	understanding
PERTINACIOUS	tenacious
PERUKE	wig
PERVIOUS	accessible
PESTIFEROUS	annoying
PETCOCK	valve
PETTIFOG	quibble
PETTISH	peevish
PHANTASMAGORIA	visions
PHILIPPIC	invective
PHILISTINE	yahoo
PHLEGMATIC	impassive
PHYSIOGNOMY	appearance

PIACULAR	sinful
PIATION	atonement
PICARESQUE	scoundrel
PICAROON	robber
PIEBALD	spotted
PIED	speckled
PILOSE	hairy
PILPUL	hairsplitting
PINGUID	fat
PIQUANT	spicy
PISCATOR	fisherman
PISHOGUE	curse
PISMIRE	ant
PLANGENT	loud
PLAUSIVE	praising
PLENIPOTENTIARY	diplomat
PLENITUDINOUS	fat
PLUPERFECT	extraordinary
PLUVIAL	rainy
PLUVIOUS	precipitating
POCOCURANTE	neglectful
POETASTER	poet
POGUE	kiss
POLEMICAL	debative
POLITY	government
POLTROON	coward
POLYDIPSIA	thirst
POLYGLOT	multilingual
POLYHISTOR	scholar
POLYONYMOUS	aliases
POLYPHAGIA	gluttony

POLYSTICHOUS	serial
POPINJAY	chatter
PORCINE	piggish
PORTENTOUS	foreshadowing
PORTMANTEAU	suitcase
POSIT	assume
POSTICHE	false
POSTPRANDIAL	after dinner
POSTULANT	novice
POTATION	drink
POTHER	fuss
PRATE	chatter
PRECIOSITY	tasteful
PRECIPITOUS	steep
PRECOCIOUS	advanced
PRECONIZE	compliment
PREDACEOUS	stalking
PREDE	plunder
PREFACTORY	preliminary
PREGUSTATION	anticipation
PREHENSILE	grasping
PREHENSION	grasping
PREMONITORY	warning
PREOCCUPATE	anticipate
PREPONDERANT	dominant
PREPOSSESSION	prejudice
PRESAGE	predict
PRESBYOPIA	farsightedness
PRESCIENT	foreknowledge
PRESCIND	separate
PRESTIGIOUS	juggling

PRETERNATURAL	supernatural
PREVENIENT	anticipatory
PRIAPIC	manly
PRIGGERY	theft
PRIGGISH	smug
PRIMORDIAL	original
PROBATIVE	proving
PROBITY	honesty
PROBOSCIS	nose
PROCÈS-VERBAL	record
PROCHEIN	nearest
PROCRUSTEAN	drastic
PROCUMBENT	lean
PROFANATION	blasphemy
PROFLIGACY	extravagant
PROFLUENT	smooth
PROFUNDITY	profound
PROFUSE	lavish
PROGENESIS	origin
PROGENITOR	ancestor
PROGENY	children
PROLEGOMENON	introduction
PROLEPSIS	anticipation
PROLIX	wordy
PROMULGE	proclaim
PROPAGATION	spreading
PROPERATE	hasten
PROPHESIER	predictor
PROPHYLACTIC	preventative
PROPINQUITY	proximity
PROPITIATE	appease

PROPITIOUS	favorable
PROROGUE	postpone
PROSAIC	dull
PROTEAN	chameleon
PROTUBERANT	spreading
PROTUBERATE	expand
PROVENDER	food
PROVENIENCE	source
PROVENLY	doubtlessly
PROVISORILY	temporarily
PRURIENT	obscene
PSELLISM	stuttering
PTYALOGOGUE	salivation
PUERILE	childish
PUERILISM	childishness
PUGILIST	boxer
PUGNACIOUS	quarrelsome
PUISSANT	strong
PULCHRITUDE	beauty
PULCHRITUDINOUS	attractive
PULE	whine
PUNCTILIOUS	punctual
PUNDIT	intellect
PURLIEUS	limits
PURLOINED	steal
PURULENT	pus-like
PURVEYOR	supplier
PUSILLANIMOUS	cowardly
PYROTIC	caustic

Q

QUAB	unfinished
QUADREL	brick
QUADRENNIAL	fourth
QUARTERN	quadrant
QUEAN	prostitute
QUENELLE	dumpling
QUERULOUS	irritable
QUIDNUNC	busybody
QUINTESSENTIAL	typical
QUISLING	traitor
QUIXOTIC	impractical
QUODLIBET	subtlety
QUOTIDIAN	ordinary

R

RACINAGE	adornment
RACONTEUR	storyteller
RAILLERY	jest
RAKISH	jaunty
RAPACIOUS	ravenous
RAPHE	seam
RAPPROCHEMENT	cordiality
RATIOCINATION	inference
RAVISH	seize
REAGENT	initiator
REBARBATIVE	irritating
RECALCITRANT	stubborn
RECENSION	revision
RECHERCHÉ	unusual
RECIDIVISM	repeated
RECIPROCITY	mutuality
RECOGNIZANCE	pledge
RECONDITE	confusing
RECREANT	turncoat
RECRUDESCENCE	return
RECTITUDINOUS	moral
RECUILEMENT	recoiling

RECUMBENT	prone
RECUSANCY	denial
REDACT	edit
REDARGUE	disprove
REDINTEGRATE	renovate
REDOLENT	fragrant
REDOUBT	fortification
REDOUBTABLE	dreaded
REDOUND	effect
REFRACTORY	stubborn
REFULGENT	luminous
REGENT	governor
REIVE	plunder
RELEXIFICATION	translation
RELIQUARY	casket
RELUCENT	reflecting
REMIT	release
REMONSTRATE	object
RENAISSANCE	rebirth
RENDITION	extraction
RENITENCY	opposition
RENITENT	resistant
REPAIR	return
REPARATION	repayment
REPARTITION	distribution
REPAST	meal
REPERTOIRE	performances
REPINE	yearning
REPLETION	fullness
REPLEVY	recovery

REPORTAGE	reporting
REPUGN	oppose
REQUIEM	dirge
REREMICE	bats
RESECTION	removal
RESIDUUM	residue
RESILE	recoil
RESTIVE	unruly
RETICULATED	netlike
RETINUE	followers
RETORTION	bend
RETROGRADE	backward
REVETMENT	embankment
REVIVIFICATION	restoration
REVIVIFY	restore
REYNARD	fox
RHABDOMANCY	divination
RHONCHUS	rale
RIBALD	profane
RIDDANCE	deliverance
RIPOSTE	insulting
RISIBLE	funny
RODOMONTADE	bragging
ROENTGEN	X-ray
ROGATION	litany
ROGUE	scoundrel
ROISTER	revel
ROUSTABOUT	worker
ROYTISH	wild
RUBRIC	title

RUCTION	quarrel
RUDIMENTARY	elementary
RUFESCENT	reddish
RUFUS	reddish
RUGOSE	wrinkled
RUMINATE	ponder
RUTILANT	ruddy

S

SABULOUS	sandy
SACCADIC	jerky
SACERDOTAL	priestly
SACHEM	leader
SAGACIOUS	perceptive
SAGACITY	wisdom
SAGITTATE	triangular
SALACIOUS	lustful
SALEBROSITY	coarseness
SALIENT	noticeable
SALTANT	dancing
SALUTARY	beneficial
SALVIFIC	saving
SANATIVE	healing
SANGFROID	imperturbability
SANGUINARY	bloody
SANGUINE	cheerful
SAPID	delicious
SAPIENCE	wisdom
SAPOR	flavor
SAPPHISM	lesbianism
SARCOPHAGUS	coffin

SARCOUS	fleshy
SARDONIC	sarcastic
SARTORIAL	tailored
SATIATE	satisfy
SATURNINE	gloomy
SAULT	waterfall
SAVOIR FAIRE	tact
SCABROUS	rough
SCARCEMENT	projection
SCATOLOGICAL	obscene
SCHISMATIC	dissenting
SCHLEMIEL	bungler
SCIENTER	knowingly
SCIOLISTIC	superficial
SCION	descendant
SCLEROSIS	hardening
SCOPULA	broom
SCOTOMA	blind spot
SCRIVENER	writer
SCROFULOUS	soiled
SCURRILOUS	abusive
SECUND	unilateral
SEDITIOUS	antigovernment
SEDULOUS	diligent
SEGUE	continual
SEIGNIORY	boss
SELCOUTH	unusual
SEMBLABLE	ostensible
SEMINAL	original
SENECTITUDE	seniorhood
SENESCENT	aging

SENSIFEROUS	sensitive
SENSORIUM	brain
SENTENTIA	maxim
SENTIENT	aware
SEPTENTRIONAL	northern
SEQUESTRATION	separation
SERAC	pinnacle
SESQUIPEDALIAN	wordy
SETACEOUS	bristled
SEVERAL	separate
SEXAGESIMAL	sixtieth
SHENDSHIP	punishment
SHIBBOLETH	slogan
SIBILANT	hissing
SIBYLLINE	prophetic
SIDEREAL	starry
SIGMATISM	mispronunciation
SIMULACRUM	pretense
SINCIPUT	forehead
SINGULAR	unique
SINUOUS	winding
SIRENIC	attractive
SKELLUM	rascal
SKIMBLE-SKAMBLE	wandering
SLUMGULLION	stew
SOBRIQUET	nickname
SODALITY	society
SOIGNÉ	sophisticated
SOIREES	parties
SOLECISM	mistake
SOLECISTIC	ungrammatical

SOLICITOUS	worried
SOLIDARY	united
SOLIPSISM	egoistic
SOLITUDINARIAN	recluse
SOMATIC	physical
SOMBROUS	somber
SOMNAMBULISM	sleepwalking
SOMNOLENT	sleepy
SONANCE	sound
SOPHISTIC	illogical
SOPHISTRY	deception
SOPORIFEROUS	asleep
SOPORIFIC	sleepy
SORORAL	sisterly
SOUBRETTE	maidservant
SOVEREIGN	supreme
SPECILLUM	probe
SPECIOUS	deceptive
SPECTATION	aspect
SPECTRAL	ghostlike
SPEET	stab
SPELUNKING	caving
SPITAL	hospital
SPLENETIC	irritable
SPLORE	carousal
SPOLIATE	steal
SPURIOUS	false
STANCHION	pillar
STASIS	inert
STENOSIS	narrowing
STENTORIAN	loud

STERTOROUS	loud
STILETTO	dagger
STOCHASTIC	random
STOLIDITY	apathy
STOUR	battle
STROBIC	spinning
STULTIFY	fool
STUPEFACTION	stupidity
STYGIAN	gloomy
SUBALTERN	subordinate
SUBLIME	glorious
SUBLUNARY	terrestrial
SUBSUMED	included
SUBULATED	pointed
SUI GENERIS	unique
SUNDER	sever
SUPERANNUATED	dated
SUPEREROGATORY	unnecessary
SUPERFLUOUS	unnecessary
SUPERLUCRATION	profit
SUPERNAL	heavenly
SUPERNUMERARY	extra
SUPPLICATE	plead
SUPPOSITITIOUS	dishonest
SUPPURATE	fester
SURCEASE	terminate
SURCREW	increase
SURPLUSAGE	surplus
SUSPIRATION	sigh
SUSTENTATION	upkeep
SUSURRATION	whisper

SUSURROUS	whispering
SVELTE	urbane
SYBARITE	wealthy
SYCOPHANTS	flatterers
SYLLOGISM	reasoning
SYMBIOSIS	mutualism
SYNCHRONISM	timetable
SYNCHRONOUS	contemporaneous
SYNERGY	combination
SYNOPTIC	comprehensive
SYNTHESIS	combination
SYSTEMIC	allover
SYSTOLE	contraction

T

TAAS	pile
TABESCENT	diminished
TACHYCARDIA	rapid heartbeat
TACHYPNEA	hyperventilation
TACITURN	silent
TACTILE	tangible
TANKARD	mug
TATTERDEMALION	ruffian
TAUROMACHY	bullfighting
TAUTOLOGICAL	repetitious
TAXONOMIST	systematist
TEGUMENT	covering
TEMERARIOUS	reckless
TEMERITY	audacity
TEMPESTIVE	seasonable
TEMPORIZE	compromise
TENDENTIOUS	biased
TENEBRIFIC	obscuring
TENEBROUS	dark
TERATOID	monsterlike
TEREBRATE	sting
TERGIVERSATION	ambiguity

TERMAGANT	nagger
TERTIARY	third
TESSELLATED	inlaid
TETCHY	irritable
THAUMATURGIC	miraculous
THAUMATURGIST	magician
THAUMATURGY	miracle
THESPIAN	actor
THEWLESS	weak
THRALL	slavery
THRALLDOM	servitude
THRENODY	lament
THROMBOSIS	clot
THYMION	wart
TIMOROUS	timid
TINTINNABULATION	ringing
TITFER	hat
TITIVATE	adorn
TITUBATION	staggering
TOCSIN	alarm
TORPID	sluggish
TORPOR	apathy
TORPORIFIC	lethargic
TOTEMIC	emblematic
TOTIPALMATE	web-footed
TRACE	path
TRACTABLE	controllable
TRADUCE	slander
TRADUCEMENT	harm
TRANSLUNARY	heavenly
TRANSMOGRIFY	transform

TRANSMUTATIONAL	conversional
TRANSMUTE	transform
TRAVERSE	penetrate
TREMULOUS	trembling
TRENCHANT	effective
TRIGAMOUS	thrice-married
TRIPLICITY	trifecta
TRISMUS	lockjaw
TRITURATE	crush
TROGLODYTIC	primitive
TROIKA	trio
TRUCULENT	quarrelsome
TRUNCATE	blunted
TUBER	swelling
TUCKET	fanfare
TUMESCENT	swollen
TUMULOSE	hilly
TURBID	muddy
TURBIDITY	cloudiness
TURBINATION	spiral
TUSSIS	cough
TYPHLOSIS	sightless
TYRO	novice

U

UBIQUITOUS	omnipresent
ULTION	revenge
ULTRA VIRES	unauthorized
ULULATE	wail
ULULATION	howling
UMBERMENT	throng
UMBRAGEOUS	shady
UNBARBED	shaven
UNBOSOM	disclose
UNCINATE	hooked
UNCTUOUS	insincere
UNEXPURGATED	unedited
UNGUENT	ointment
UNREQUITED	unreturned
URSINE	bearlike
USTULATION	heating
USURY	interest
UTILITARIANISM	usefulness
UVULA	lobe
UXORIOUS	submissive

V

VACUOUS	empty
VAGARY	impulse
VAGINATE	sheathed
VAGROM	vagrant
VAINGLORIOUS	perplexed
VALETUDINARIAN	invalid
VALIANCE	valor
VANGUARD	forefront
VASSALAGE	servitude
VATICINATION	prediction
VELDT	grassland
VELLEITY	wish
VELLUM	parchment
VENAL	bribable
VENALITY	corruption
VENENATE	poison
VENEREOUS	lustful
VENERER	hunter
VENIAL	pardonable
VERIDICAL	truthful
VERISIMILITUDE	truth
VERMICULATE	dishonest

VERNAL	spring
VERTIGINOUS	whirling
VESICANT	blister
VESTMENT	robe
VICINAL	near
VICISSITUDINOUS	changeable
VIDUITY	widowhood
VIGNERON	winegrower
VILIPEND	revile
VIRAGO	shrew
VIRIDITY	youth
VIRULIFEROUS	infectious
VISCEROTONIC	happy-go-lucky
VISCID	sticky
VITIATE	nullify
VITREOUS	glassy
VITRIOLIC	biting
VITUPERATION	criticism
VIVA VOCE	orally
VOCIFEROUSNESS	outcry
VOLUPTUARY	sensual
VOTARIES	followers
VOUCHSAFE	condescend
VULPINE	crafty

W

WAGGERY	trick
WAGGISH	funny
WAMBLE	stagger
WASSAIL	toast
WASTAGE	erosion
WELTER	jumble
WIDDERSHINS	counterclockwise
WONTED	ordinary
WRAITH	ghost

W

X

XANTHIC	yellow
XANTHIPPE	shrew
X-AXIS	axis
XEBEC	ship
XENOPHOBIC	antiforeign
XERIC	dry
XYLOID	woody
XYLOSE	sugar

Y

YAMMER	whine
Y-AXIS	axis
YEGG	robber
YERK	thrash
YEUKY	itchy
YOKEMATE	coworker
YOUNKER	gentlemen
YURT	tent

Z

ZABERNISM	bullying
ZENANA	harem
ZEPHYR	breeze
ZOILIST	nagger
ZOOID	animal
ZOOPHORIC	animal-like
ZUCCHETTO	skullcap
ZYME	ferment
ZYMURGY	fermentation

common words to COMPLEX WORDS

a

abnormal	ANOMALOUS
absorbent	BIBULOUS
absorption	OSMOSIS
abstinent	ASCETIC
abusive	SCURRILOUS
accessible	PERVIOUS
accessory	ACCOUTREMENT
accessory	ANCILLA
accessory	APPURTENANCE
accidental	ADVENTITIOUS
accompanying	APPURTENANT
accompanying	CONCOMITANT
accomplishable	FACILE
accord	CONSONANCE
acquit	EXCULPATE
across	ATHWART
active	KINETIC
actor	THESPIAN
adage	APHORISM
addiction	NARCOMANIA
addition	INTERCALATION

additional	ADSCITITIOUS
adjacent	JUXTAPOSED
adjoining	COUNTERMINOUS
adjure	CONJURE
admonished	IMPUGNED
adorn	TITIVATE
adornment	HONESTATION
adornment	RACINAGE
advance	ANABASIS
advanced	PRECOCIOUS
advice	PARENESIS
advocate	PARACLETE
afraid	AFFRIGHTED
after dinner	POSTPRANDIAL
afterlife	ESCHATOLOGY
aging	SENESCENT
agitated	AQUIVER
agitated	FLURRIED
agrarian	GEOPONIC
agreeable	COMPLAISANT
agreeing	CONSENTANEOUS
airy	ETHEREAL
alacrity	LEGERITY
alarm	TOCSIN
alcoholic	DIPSOMANIAC
aliases	POLYONYMOUS
allegory	APOLOGUE
allover	SYSTEMIC
all-powerful	CUNCTIPOTENT
aloofness	FROIDEUR

alter	CAPONIZE
ambiguity	TERGIVERSATION
ambush	AMBUSCADE
amorous	AMATIVE
analogous	ANALOG
analyze	ANATOMIZE
ancestor	PROGENITOR
ancient	ANTEDILUVIAN
anesthetic	ANODYNE
animal	ZOOID
animal-like	ZOOPHORIC
annoying	PESTIFEROUS
annulment	OBROGATION
ant	PISMIRE
anticipate	PREOCCUPATE
anticipation	PREGUSTATION
anticipation	PROLEPSIS
anticipatory	PREVENIENT
antiforeign	XENOPHOBIC
antigovernment	INCIVISM
antigovernment	SEDITIOUS
apart	ABSTRACT
apathy	STOLIDITY
apathy	TORPOR
appearance	PHYSIOGNOMY
appease	PROPITIATE
appendages	ADNEXA
appointment	ASSIGNATION
approve	HOMOLOGATE
argumentative	ERISTIC

aristocracy	PATRICIATE
armchair	FAUTEUIL
arousing	EROGENOUS
arrogance	MEGALOMANIA
arrogant	DEIGNOUS
artificial	ERSATZ
artificial	FACTITIOUS
asleep	SOPORIFEROUS
aspect	SPECTATION
assail	OPPUGN
assistance	CONCERTATION
assistant	COADJUTOR
assortment	ANTHOLOGY
assume	POSIT
atone	EXPIATE
atonement	PIATION
attractive	ILLECEBROUS
attractive	NUBILE
attractive	PULCHRITUDINOUS
attractive	SIRENIC
attribution	ASCRIPTION
audacity	TEMERITY
audience	ECCLESIA
authoritative	FACULTATIVE
authority	HEGEMONY
autopsy	NECROPSY
avert	AVERRUNCATE
avert	FORFEND
awakening	ENTELECHY
awakening	EPIPHANY

awakening	INCIPIENT
aware	SENTIENT
awkward	MALADROIT
axis	X-AXIS
axis	Y-AXIS

b

backward	RETROGRADE
bacterium	BACILLUS
bacterium	PATHOGEN
bad	NEFARIOUS
balanced	EQUIPONDERANT
banter	PERSIFLAGE
barge	BUCENTAUR
barter	NIFFER
bat	NOCTULE
bats	REREMICE
battle	STOUR
battlement	BRETESSE
beaded	MONILIFORM
beaming	EFFULGENT
bearlike	URSINE
beating	BASTINADO
beauty	PULCHRITUDE
beg	IMPORTUNE
beggar	MENDICANT
beginner	ABECEDARIAN
beginning	EXORDIUM
beginnings	INCUNABULA

behavior	COMPORTMENT
belch	ERUCT
believable	COLORABLE
bell tower	CLOCHER
belt	BANDOLIER
belt	CINCTURE
bend	GENUFLECT
bend	RETORTION
beneficial	SALUTARY
betroth	DESPONSATE
bewitch	ENSORCEL
bewitch	MALEFICIATE
biased	TENDENTIOUS
billion	MILLIARD
birthing	ACCOUCHEMENT
biting	ACIDULOUS
biting	MORDACIOUS
biting	MORDANT
biting	VITRIOLIC
bitter	ACRID
blackhead	COMEDO
blame	INCULPATE
blasphemy	PROFANATION
bleaching	DEALBATION
blemish	MACULATE
blending	CONFLATION
blessing	BENISON
blindness	ABLEPSIA
blind spot	SCOTOMA
blink	NICTITATE
blissful	BEATIFIC

blissful	ELYSIAN
blister	VESICANT
blood relation	CONSANGUINITY
bloody	SANGUINARY
blue	AERUGINOUS
blue	CERULEAN
blunt	OBTUSE
blunted	TRUNCATE
blurring	HALATION
boasting	GASCONADING
boasting	JACTATION
boats	BATEAUX
bold	AUDACIOUS
bold	MALAPERT
bombastic	GRANDILOQUENT
bombastic	MAGNILOQUENT
bond	LIGATION
bony	OSSEAN
book collector	BIBLIOPHILE
bookseller	BIBLIOPOLE
boorish	CHURLISH
boorish	LOUTISH
boots	GAMASHES
boredom	ENNUI
borrow	CADGE
boss	SEIGNIORY
bountiful	MUNIFICENT
boxer	PUGILIST
braggart	FANFARON
bragging	RODOMONTADE
brain	SENSORIUM

breeze	ZEPHYR
bribable	VENAL
bribe	GRATULANCE
brick	QUADREL
brief	CADUCOUS
bright	LAMBENT
bright	LUCENT
brightness	CORUSCATION
brilliance	EFFULGENCE
bristled	SETACEOUS
broom	BESOM
broom	SCOPULA
bruise	ECCHYMOSIS
brushwood	FASCINE
bubbling	EBULLITION
bullfighting	TAUROMACHY
bullying	ZABERNISM
bungler	SCHLEMIEL
burden	ENCUMBRANCE
burn	DEFLAGRATE
burned	ADUST
burp	ERUCTATE
bus	JITNEY
business	OPEROSENESS
busybody	QUIDNUNC
buttocks	FUNDAMENT
buttocks	HEINIE
buying	EMPTION

callous	INDURATE
calm	HALCYON
calming	ATARACTIC
cancer	CARCINOMA
cannibalism	ANTHROPOPHAGY
car	FLIVVER
carousal	SPLORE
cashless	ILLIQUID
casket	RELIQUARY
category	GENRE
catharsis	ABREACTION
cathedral	PANTHEON
cathouse	BAGNIO
cause	ETIOLOGY
caustic	PYROTIC
caution	CHARINESS
cautious	CHARY
caving	SPELUNKING
cavity	ALVEOLUS
chameleon	PROTEAN
champion	KEMP
chance	PERADVENTURE

change	DEDIFFERENTIATION
change	DIALAGE
changeable	MUTABLE
changeable	VICISSITUDINOUS
chanting	INCANTATION
chaperone	DUENNA
charged	IONIZED
charitable	ELEEMOSYNARY
charm	AMULET
charring	INTUMESCENT
chastity	CONTINENCE
chat	CONFABULATE
chatter	PALAVER
chatter	POPINJAY
chatter	PRATE
cheat	COZEN
cheek	BUCCAL
cheerful	SANGUINE
cheesy	CASEOUS
chew	MASTICATE
childbirth	PARTURITION
childish	PUERILE
childishness	PUERILISM
children	PROGENY
chilly	GELID
circle-like	CIRCUMFERENTIAL
clay	BRASQUE
cleanse	BOWDLERIZE
clear	LIMPID
cliff	ESCARPMENT
clock	HOROLOGE

clockwise	DEASIL
closeness	COSTIVENESS
closing	OBTURATION
clot	THROMBOSIS
clothe	ACCOUTRE
clothing	HABILIMENT
cloud	NIMBUS
cloud	NUBILATE
cloudiness	TURBIDITY
club	CUDGEL
clumsy	LOUT
coarseness	SALEBROSITY
coffin	SARCOPHAGUS
coinlike	NUMMULAR
coldness	ALGIDITY
collar	COLLET
collector	ANTIQUARIAN
combination	SYNERGY
combination	SYNTHESIS
comic	HARLEQUIN
command	MANDAMUS
commonplace	PEDESTRIAN
communicant	DEIPNOSOPHIST
compensate	COUNTERVAIL
complain	KVETCH
complaining	CARPING
complete	ARRANT
compliment	PRECONIZE
composite	MONTAGE
comprehensive	SYNOPTIC
compromise	TEMPORIZE

conceal	PALLIATE
concise	EPIGRAMMATIC
conciseness	BRACHYLOGY
conclusion	PERORATION
concubine	ODALISQUE
condescend	VOUCHSAFE
conductor	IMPRESARIO
confess	INTROMIT
confidential	ESOTERIC
confirmation	HOMOLOGATION
confiscate	ESCHEAT
conforming	CANONICAL
confuse	BEMUSE
confuse	OBFUSCATE
confused	FLUMMOXED
confusing	ABSTRUSE
confusing	RECONDITE
confusion	ENIGMA
confusion	GALIMATIAS
confusion	OBNUBILATION
confusion	OBSCURANTISM
connecting	ANNECTENT
conquering	DEBELLATION
considering	LISTENABLE
constipation	OBSTIPATION
constrictive	ASTRINGENT
contaminate	ADULTERATE
contemporaneous	COEVAL
contemporaneous	SYNCHRONOUS
contemporary	MODERNITY
contiguous	CONTERMINOUS

continual	SEGUE
continuance	PERMANSION
contraction	SYSTOLE
contributory	ADJUVANT
controllable	TRACTABLE
conversation	INTERLOCUTION
conversional	TRANSMUTATIONAL
convincing	COGENT
cooling	DEFERVESCENCE
cooperation	COLLEGIALITY
copy	APOGRAPH
cordiality	RAPPROCHEMENT
corruption	VENALITY
cough	TUSSIS
counterclockwise	WIDDERSHINS
courteousness	COMITY
courtly	AULIC
covering	PANOPLY
covering	TEGUMENT
coward	POLTROON
cowardly	CRAVEN
cowardly	PUSILLANIMOUS
coworker	YOKEMATE
crackling	CREPITATION
crafty	VULPINE
crater	CALDERA
craving	APPETENCE
crescent	DEMILUNE
crevices	INTERSTICES
critical	CENSORIOUS
criticism	DIATRIBE

criticism	VITUPERATION
criticize	ABRADE
criticize	CASTIGATE
criticize	EXCORIATE
crossing	DECUSSATE
crucial	CLIMACTERIC
cruel	DISPITEOUS
crush	TRITURATE
crying	LACRIMAL
culmination	APOGEE
culmination	PERIGEE
cupid	AMORETTO
cure-all	PANACEA
curse	ANATHEMA
curse	IMPRECATION
curse	MALEDICTION
curse	PISHOGUE
curt	LACONIC
curtain	CORTINA
curved	AQUILINE
customary	CONSUETUDINARY

d

dagger	STILETTO
daily	DIURNAL
dance	DANDLE
dancing	SALTANT
dangerous	PARLOUS
dark	APHOTIC
dark	CALIGINOUS
dark	TENEBROUS
darken	OBNUBILATE
darkening	OBSCURATION
dated	SUPERANNUATED
day and night	NYCHTHEMERON
dead	NECROTIC
debate	DISPUTATION
debative	POLEMICAL
decade	DECENNIUM
deceit	INGANNATION
deception	SOPHISTRY
deceptive	DELUSIVE
deceptive	SPECIOUS
deceptiveness	CASUISTRY
defamer	DENIGRATOR

defense	MUNIMENT
definition	CIRCUMSCRIPTION
degeneration	DEVOLUTION
dejection	CONTRISTATION
delay	LACHES
delicious	SAPID
deliverance	RIDDANCE
denial	ABNEGATION
denial	RECUSANCY
denounce	FULMINATE
dense	IMPOROUS
deny	GAINSAY
depressed	ABJECT
deprivation	DISESTABLISHMENT
deprive	EVISCERATE
depriver	DISESTABLISHMENTARIAN
descendant	SCION
deserved	MERITOCRATIC
desire	OPTATE
desiring	ORECTIC
desk	ESCRITOIRE
destroy	EXTIRPATE
destroy	INTERDICT
destroyer	ICONOCLAST
destructive	PERNICIOUS
detestable	EXECRATIVE
detested	EXECRATED
deviating	AWRY
dialect	IDIOM
dictionary	LEXICON
digression	DIVAGATION

diligent	ASSIDUOUS
diligent	SEDULOUS
dim	CREPUSCULAR
diminished	TABESCENT
diplomat	PLENIPOTENTIARY
direct	INCISIVE
dirge	EQUICEDE
dirge	REQUIEM
disappearance	LYSIS
disapproval	DISAPPROBATION
disarray	DISHABILLE
discipline	FERULE
disclose	UNBOSOM
discord	DISSONANCE
discussion	DISQUISITION
disease-causing	IATROGENIC
diseased	PANDEMIC
diseased	PATHOGENIC
disgrace	OBLOQUY
disgrace	OPPROBRIUM
disgusting	FULSOME
disgusting	FURCIFEROUS
dishonest	MENDACIOUS
dishonest	SUPPOSITITIOUS
dishonest	VERMICULATE
dislike	ANTIPATHY
dislocation	LUXATION
disloyalty	APOSTASY
dismiss	CASHIER
disobedient	CONTUMACIOUS
disorder	ENTROPY

disparagement	EPITHET
disparaging	PEJORATIVE
disprove	REDARGUE
disputation	CONFUTATION
dispute	CONTESTATION
dispute	ELENCHUS
disputing	CHOPLOGIC
disregard	IMPUDENCE
dissent	DISSIDENCE
dissenting	SCHISMATIC
distinct	DISPARATE
distortion	ANAMORPHOSIS
distribution	REPARTITION
distrustfully	ASKANCE
disuse	DESUETUDE
diverseness	MULTIFARIOUSNESS
divide	BIFURCATE
divination	RHABDOMANCY
divine	NUMINOUS
division	CANTON
division	DICHOTOMY
division	PARTITION
dominant	PREPONDERANT
double-edged	ANCIPITAL
doubtlessly	PROVENLY
downward	DECLIVITY
drastic	PROCRUSTEAN
draw	LIMN
dreaded	REDOUBTABLE
dreary	DRIEGH
dried	DESICCATE

drink	POTATION
drowsy	OSCITANT
drunken	BACCHANALIAN
drunkenness	INTEMPERANCE
dry	EXSUCCOUS
dry	XERIC
dull	PROSAIC
dullness	HEBETUDE
dumbness	CRASSITUDE
dumpling	QUENELLE
dying	MORIBUND

e

eagerness	ALACRITY
eagerness	AVIDITY
earwax	CERUMEN
eastern	ORTIVE
edible	COMESTIBLE
edible	ESCULENT
edit	EMEND
edit	EXPURGATE
edit	REDACT
education	HYPNOPEDIA
effect	REDOUND
effective	EFFLICACIOUS
effective	TRENCHANT
effeminate	EPICENE
eggplant	AUBERGINE
egoistic	SOLIPSISM
election	COOPTION
electric	GALVANIC
elementary	RUDIMENTARY
eloquence	LOQUENCE
eloquent	EUPHUISTIC
emanation	EFFLUVIUM

emancipation	MANUMISSION
embankment	REVETMENT
embarrassing	CONTUMELIOUS
embarrassment	CONTRETEMPS
embarrassment	DISCOMFITURE
embezzlement	DEFALCATION
embezzlement	PECULATION
emblematic	TOTEMIC
embodiment	AVATAR
empty	INANE
empty	VACUOUS
enclose	INTUSSUSCEPT
enclose	INVAGINATE
encourage	INSPIRIT
encouraging	EXHORTATORY
encouraging	HORTATIVE
encumbrance	FARDEL
end	CLOTURE
ending	DECRESCENT
endowment	APPANAGE
endowment	DOTATION
enhancement	LIONIZATION
enlarge	AUGMENT
enlargement	ELEPHANTIASIS
enlarging	ACCRESCENT
ensnaring	ILLAQUEATION
entanglement	IMBROGLIO
environment	MILIEU
equal	EGALITARIAN
equipment	EQUIPAGE
equivalent	EQUIPOLLENT

erosion	WASTAGE
error	CORRIGENDUM
errorless	DISABUSED
erupting	DISSILIENT
escape	ABSQUATULATE
escape	AVOLATE
essential	GRAVAMEN
eulogy	PANEGYRIC
evening	CREPUSCULE
evergreen	CONIFER
everlasting	ETERNE
evict	DETURBATE
evildoer	MALEFACTOR
evil spirit	CACODEMON
exaggeration	FUSTIAN
exaggeration	HYPERBOLE
exaggeration	MYTHOMANIA
excellent	EXIMIOUS
excess	ACRASIA
excited	DITHYRAMBIC
exhaustion	DELASSATION
exhaustion	INANITION
exodus	HEGIRA
expand	PROTUBERATE
expanding	DILATANT
expert	COGNOSCENTE
expert	MAVIN
explanation	EXCLAMATION
explanation	EXEGESIS
explanatory	EXEGETICAL
exposed	PATULOUS

externalize	HYPOSTATIZE
extra	SUPERNUMERARY
extraction	RENDITION
extraordinary	PLUPERFECT
extravagant	PROFLIGACY

f

faithlessness	PERFIDY
faker	MALINGERER
false	APOCRYPHAL
false	POSTICHE
false	SPURIOUS
falsehood	PARALOGISM
fanfare	TUCKET
fare	FERRIAGE
farmer	HUSBANDMAN
farsightedness	PRESBYOPIA
fastening	COAPTATION
fat	CORPULENT
fat	PINGUID
fat	PLENITUDINOUS
father	PATERFAMILIAS
fatigue	LASSITUDE
fault-finding	CAPTIOUS
favorable	PROPITIOUS
fearless	INTREPID
feces	EXCREMENT
feeble	IMPUISSANCE
ferment	ZYME

fermentation	ZYMURGY
fertile	FECUND
fertility	FECUNDITY
fester	SUPPURATE
feverless	AFEBRILE
fiber	JUTE
fidelity	FEALTY
fierce	LEONINE
figurative	ALLEGORICAL
finger	DACTYL
fireball	CORPOSANT
firm	ADAMANTINE
fisherman	PISCATOR
fit	PAROXYSM
flag	FANION
flame	FLAMBEAU
flash	FULGURATION
flask	COSTREL
flatter	INVEIGLE
flatterers	SYCOPHANTS
flattering	ADULATORY
flattering	GNATHONIC
flattery	FLUMMERY
flatulent	BORBORYGMUS
flavor	SAPOR
flavoring	CLARY
fleet	ARGOSY
fleeting	FUGACIOUS
fleshy	SARCOUS
flippant	FACETIOUS
flirtatious	COQUETTISH

floating	NATANT
flow	EXTRAVASATE
flowery	FLORID
flowing	CIRCUMFLUENT
follower	EPIGONE
follower	LIEGE
followers	RETINUE
followers	VOTARIES
food	ALIMENT
food	PROVENDER
fool	GOMEREL
fool	HAVEREL
fool	NODDY
fool	STULTIFY
foolish	FATUOUS
forefront	VANGUARD
forehead	SINCIPUT
foreign	HETEROCHTHONOUS
foreknowledge	PRESCIENT
foreshadow	ADUMBRATE
foreshadowing	PORTENTOUS
forgetful	DISTRAIT
forgetfulness	OBLIVESCENCE
formless	INCORPOREAL
fortification	BREASTWORK
fortification	DEFILADE
fortification	REDOUBT
fossil	CONODONT
foul	FECULENT
fourth	QUADRENNIAL
fox	REYNARD

fractional	ALIQUOT
fragile	FRANGIBLE
fragment	ODDMENT
fragranced	MYRRHED
fragrant	REDOLENT
frantic	FRENETIC
fraud	OBREPTION
free	MANUMIT
frenzied	CORYBANTIC
friendly	CONVIVIAL
friendly	GREGARIOUS
frighten	GLOPPEN
frigid	HYPERBOREAN
frugal	PARSIMONIOUS
fulfillment	EFFLORESCENCE
fulfillment	INDULGENCE
fullness	REPLETION
funeral rite	OBSEQUY
funny	RISIBLE
funny	WAGGISH
fuss	POTHER

g

gallery	CLERESTORY
gather	COLLOCATE
gather	IMPOSTUMATE
gaudy	BEDIZEN
gaudy	MERETRICIOUS
generosity	LARGESSE
gentleman	YOUNKER
gentleness	LENITY
gentleness	MANSUETUDE
germless	ASEPTIC
ghastly	CADAVEROUS
ghost	WRAITH
ghostlike	SPECTRAL
ghostly	CHTHONIC
giant	ACROMEGALY
glassy	VITREOUS
glide	GLISSADE
gloomy	ATRABILIOUS
gloomy	SATURNINE
gloomy	STYGIAN
glorious	SUBLIME
glutton	GOURMAND

gluttonous	CRAPULOUS
gluttonous	EDACIOUS
gluttonous	GULOSITOUS
gluttony	CRAPULENCE
gluttony	POLYPHAGIA
goddess	DIVA
god-man	DEMIGOD
gourd	CALABASH
government	POLITY
governor	REGENT
granite	GNEISS
grasping	PREHENSILE
grasping	PREHENSION
grassland	VELDT
grassy	GRAMINEOUS
gratuity	CUMSHAW
graveyard	NECROPOLIS
grayish	CANESCENT
greed	CUPIDITY
greedy	AVARICIOUS
greedy	CUPIDINOUS
greedy	ESURIENT
greenhouse	CONSERVATORY
groin	INGUINAL
group	CABAL
group	COTERIE
growth	HISTOGENESIS
gruesome	MACABRE
guide	CICERONE
gunfire	FUSILLADE

h

habitual	INVETERATE
hairsplitting	PILPUL
hairy	HIRSUTE
hairy	LANUGINOUS
hairy	PILOSE
half	MOIETY
halitosis	OZOSTOMIA
handwritten	HOLOGRAPHIC
happiness	EUDEMONIA
happy	JOCUND
happy-go-lucky	VISCEROTONIC
harborless	IMPORTUOUS
hard	CEMENTITIOUS
harden	OSSIFY
hardened	INDURATED
hardening	SCLEROSIS
hardwood	DECIDUOUS
harem	ZENANA
harm	TRADUCEMENT
harmful	BALEFUL
harmful	MALEFIC
harmful	NOCUOUS

harmless	INNOCUOUS
harmony	CONCINNITY
harshness	ACRIMONY
harshness	CACOPHONY
hasten	PROPERATE
hastening	FESTINATE
hat	CALPAC
hat	TITFER
hateful	ODIBLE
hatred	MISANTHROPY
hatred	ODIUM
haughtiness	HAUTEUR
headband	DIADEM
healed	CICATRIZED
healing	SANATIVE
heap	AGGERATE
heating	CALEFACIENT
heating	USTULATION
heaven	EMPYREAN
heavenly	SUPERNAL
heavenly	TRANSLUNARY
hell	PERDITION
henchman	MYRMIDON
hermit	ANCHORITE
hermit	EREMITE
heroic	HOMERIC
hidden	ABDITIVE
hidden	FULIGINOUS
hilly	TUMULOSE
hissing	SIBILANT
historian	ANNALIST

hold	INTELLECTION
homesickness	NOSTOMANIA
homosexuality	HOMOEROTICISM
honesty	PROBITY
hooked	UNCINATE
horn	CERAS
horrible	EGREGIOUS
horse	HOUYHNHNM
horsemanship	MANÈGE
hospital	SPITAL
hostile	OPPUGNANT
hound	HUNTCOUNTER
howling	ULULATION
hub	CYNOSURE
huge	BROBDINGNAGIAN
huge	CYCLOPEAN
hum	BOMBINATE
humanistic	ANTHROPOMORPHIC
hunter	VENERER
hymnal	ANTIPHONAL
hyperventilation	ANHELATION
hyperventilation	TACHYPNEA
hypnotism	BRAIDISM

i

ideal	APOTHEOSIS
identical	ISOMORPHIC
idle	OTIOSE
idleness	OTIOSITY
idol	MAUMET
idolatry	IMPIETY
ignorance	NESCIENCE
ill health	CACHEXIA
illiteracy	ALEXIA
illogical	SOPHISTIC
illusion	CHIMERA
imaginary	CHIMERICAL
imaginary	EIDOLON
imitation	ONOMATOPOEIA
imitation	PARODY
imitative	MIMETIC
immaterial	IMMATERIATE
immerse	DEMERGE
immortality	ATHANASIA
impassive	PHLEGMATIC
imperturbability	SANGFROID
impractical	QUIXOTIC

imprisoned	IMMURED
improve	AMELIORATE
impulse	MEGRIM
impulse	VAGARY
impulsive	CAPRICIOUS
inappropriateness	MALAPROPISM
inbreeding	HOMOGAMY
incidentally	OBITER
included	SUBSUMED
inclusion	IRREDENTISM
incomplete	INCHOATE
incomprehension	APHASIA
incongruous	OXYMORON
inconsistent	INCONSONANT
inconvenient	INCOMMODIOUS
increase	SURCREW
incurable	IMMEDICABLE
independence	AUTARKY
independently	AUTOGENOUSLY
independently	ENDOGENOUS
indescribable	INENARRABLE
indigestion	DYSPEPSIA
indirect	AMBAGE
indirectness	OBLIQUITY
indistinct	OBLITERATIVE
indistinguishable	FUNGIBLE
indulgent	APOLAUSTIC
inert	STASIS
infatuate	INSENSATE
infectious	VIRULIFEROUS
inference	ILLATION

inference	RATIOCINATION
inferior	DRECK
inflexible	OBDURATE
inheritance	HEREDITAMENT
inheritance	PATRIMONY
initiator	REAGENT
inlaid	TESSELLATED
insatiable	INSATIATE
inseparable	INDISCERPTIBLE
insert	INTERCALATE
insert	INTERPOLATE
insight	APERCUS
insincere	DISINGENUOUS
insincere	UNCTUOUS
insoluble	HYDROPHOBIC
inspiration	AFFLATUS
inspired	ORACULAR
instruction	MANUDUCTION
insulting	INVECTIVE
insulting	RIPOSTE
integration	CONCATENATION
intellect	PUNDIT
intellectual	NOETIC
interest	USURY
interrupt	OBTRUDE
intersperse	INTERLARDED
introduction	PROLEGOMENON
introvert	NEBBISH
invade	FILIBUSTER
invalid	VALETUDINARIAN
invective	PHILIPPIC

inward	CENTRIPETAL
iridescent	OPALESCENT
ironic	ANTIPHRASTIC
irrefutable	APODICTIC
irrefutable	IRREFRAGABLE
irregularity	ANOMALY
irresistible	INELUCTABLE
irritable	CHOLERIC
irritable	QUERULOUS
irritable	SPLENETIC
irritable	TETCHY
irritating	REBARBATIVE
isolate	ENISLE
itchy	YEUKY
itinerant	PERIPATETIC

j

jaunty	RAKISH
jerky	SACCADIC
jest	RAILLERY
join	INOSCULATE
joining	CHAMPERTOUS
joint	PARCENARY
joke	JOCOSERIOUS
joker	FARCEUR
journey	PEREGRINATION
juggling	PRESTIGIOUS
jumble	WELTER

k

kill	INTERNECINE
kin	COGNATE
kind	BENIGNANT
kingpin	KINGBOLT
kiss	OSCULATION
kiss	POGUE
knife	KNOUT
knife	KWAIKEN
knot	COCKADE
knottiness	GENICULATION
knowingly	SCIENTER

L

laborious	OPEROSE
lament	THRENODY
lamp	LUCERN
last	PERDURE
laugh	CACHINNATE
laugh	FLEER
lavish	PROFUSE
law book	CUSTUMAL
laxative	APERIENT
lazy	FAINÉANT
lazy	INDOLENT
leader	SACHEM
leaderless	INTERREGNUM
lean	PROCUMBENT
left	LARBOARD
legal	CONGEABLE
legislator	NOMOTHETE
lesbianism	SAPPHISM
lethargic	TORPORIFIC
letters	EPISTOLARY
levels	ECHELONS
lewd	LICENTIOUSNESS

lie	CANARD
lighthearted	INSOUCIANT
lightless	FUSCOUS
lightless	OPAQUE
limb	HEPTACOLIC
limits	PURLIEUS
limp	FLACCID
limping	CLAUDICATION
linen	CAMBRIC
linen-like	BYSSACEOUS
link	CATENATE
link	NEXUS
listening	AUSCULTATION
listless	LANGUOROUS
litany	ROGATION
litigiousness	BARRATRY
loan	IMPREST
loaning	MUTUATION
lobe	UVULA
local	INSULAR
localized	ENDEMIC
lockjaw	TRISMUS
logical	DIALECTIC
longevity	MACROBIOSIS
long-sided	LONGILATERAL
lordly	IMPERIOUS
lot	CABOODLE
loud	PLANGENT
loud	STENTORIAN
loud	STERTOROUS
lover	INAMORATA

lullaby	BERCEUSE
luminous	REFULGENT
luster	GLISTER
lustful	HIRCINE
lustful	ITHYPALLIC
lustful	LASCIVIOUS
lustful	LIBIDINOUS
lustful	SALACIOUS
lustful	VENEREOUS
lying	PERJURIOUS

m

magic	GRAMARYE
magical	HERMETIC
magician	THAUMATURGIST
magnolia-like	MAGNOLIACEOUS
maidservant	SOUBRETTE
malaria	PALUDISM
malicious	MALEVOLENT
malignity	LIVOR
man-hater	MISANDRIST
manly	PRIAPIC
manure	MUCK
mapper	CARTOGRAPHER
marital	CONNUBIAL
matchless	INIMITABLE
maxim	SENTENTIA
meager	EXIGUOUS
meal	REPAST
meandering	EXCURSIVE
meat-eating	CARNIVOROUS
meeting	CONVENTICLE
melodic	CANOROUS
melodiously	DULCETLY

melt	DELIQUESCE
memorial	CAIRN
memory aid	MNEMONIC
mercenary	CONDOTTIERE
merging	AMALGAMATION
merited	CONDIGN
merry	BLITHE
meticulousness	ANALITY
middle-class	BOURGEOIS
midget	HOMUNCULUS
mimicking	ECHOPRAXIA
miracle	THAUMATURGY
miraculous	THAUMATURGIC
mispronunciation	SIGMATISM
misspeak	MISAVER
mistake	SOLECISM
mistaken	PECCABLE
misunderstanding	MALENTENDU
misunderstanding	MISPRISION
misunderstood	IMPERCIPIENT
mitigative	PALLIATIVE
mixed	ECLECTIC
mixed	HETEROGENEOUS
mixture	MÉLANGE
mobocracy	OCHLOCRACY
model	PARAGON
moderate	ABSTEMIOUS
mold	MATRIX
momentous	MOLIMINOUS
money	FIVER
monsterlike	TERATOID

moral	IMPUTRESCIBLE
moral	RECTITUDINOUS
morality	DEONTOLOGY
morning	MATINAL
motion	KINESIS
mournful	DOLOROUS
mournful	ELEGICAL
mournful	FUNEREAL
mournful	LUGUBRIOUS
mouth	EMBOUCHURE
move	DECAMP
muddy	TURBID
mug	TANKARD
multilingual	POLYGLOT
muscular	KINESTHETIC
mushroom	CHAMPIGNON
musky	MOSCHATE
musty	FROWSTY
mute	OBMUTESCENT
mutualism	SYMBIOSIS
mutuality	RECIPROCITY
mysterious	ARCANE
mysterious	INSCRUTABLE
mystical	ANAGOGIC
mystical	GNOSIS

n

nagger	TERMAGANT
nagger	ZOILIST
nagging	GROUSING
name	APPELLATION
name	MONIKER
narrowing	STENOSIS
nationalism	JINGOISM
native	AUTOCHTHONOUS
native	INDIGENOUS
natural	FERAL
naturalization	ENDENIZATION
near	VICINAL
nearest	PROCHEIN
necessarily	PERFORCE
neckline	DÉCOLLETAGE
needlelike	ACEROSE
needlelike	ACICULAR
neglectful	POCOCURANTE
nerve	EFFRONTERY
nervousness	DYSPHORIA
netlike	RETICULATED
new	NASCENT

new	NEOTERIC
niches	COLUMBARIUM
nickname	SOBRIQUET
nightmare	INCUBUS
nimble	LISSOME
nod	NUTATION
nondevelopment	AGENESIA
nonmetal	METALLOID
nonsense	DRIVEL
northern	SEPTENTRIONAL
nose	PROBOSCIS
noticeable	SALIENT
nourishing	ALIMENTARY
novice	POSTULANT
novice	TYRO
nuclei	KARYOGAMY
nullify	VITIATE
number	COEFFICIENT
number	PAGINATE
nun	CLOISTRESS

O

obesity	ADIPOSITY
object	EXPOSTULATE
object	REMONSTRATE
objection	EXPOSTULATION
obligation	OBSTRICTION
obnoxious	INVIDIOUS
obscene	LUBRICIOUS
obscene	PRURIENT
obscene	SCATOLOGICAL
obscenity	COPROLALIA
obscuring	TENEBRIFIC
observation	INVIGILATION
obstinateness	INTRACTABILITY
oceanic	PELAGIC
oddly	HUMORSOMELY
ode	EPITHALAMIUM
offering	OBLATION
official	MANDARIN
oil receptive	OLEOPHILIC
oil repellant	OLEOPHOBIC
oily	LUBRICITY
oily	OLEAGINOUS

ointment	UNGUENT
omnipresent	UBIQUITOUS
oniony	ALLIACEOUS
opening	APERTURE
opening	DEHISCENT
opening	ORIFICE
openwork	FILIGREE
oppose	REPUGN
opposite	ANTITHESIS
opposition	RENITENCY
orally	VIVA VOCE
ordinary	BANAL
ordinary	QUOTIDIAN
ordinary	WONTED
origin	PROGENESIS
original	ARCHETYPE
original	PRIMORDIAL
original	SEMINAL
ornate	BAROQUE
orthodox	ESTABLISHMENTARIAN
ostensible	SEMBLABLE
outcry	VOCIFEROUSNESS
outflow	EFFLUENCE
outline	CONSPECTUS
outline	LINEAMENT
overlapping	OBVOLUTE
overweight	ABDOMINOUS

p

pacify	MOLLIFY
paired	BINATE
paneling	BOISERIE
parchment	VELLUM
pardonable	VENIAL
parties	SOIREES
partitionable	DISCERPTIBLE
passage	FISTULA
passionate	EPITHYMETIC
path	TRACE
patience	LONGANIMITY
pattern	PARADIGM
peaceful	IRENIC
peculiarity	IDIOSYNCRACY
peerless	NONPAREIL
peevish	PETTISH
penalty	AMERCEMENT
penetrate	TRAVERSE
penmanship	CHIROGRAPHY
perceptive	SAGACIOUS
perforated	CRIBRIFORM
performances	REPERTOIRE

performers	ENSEMBLE
perfume	OLIBANUM
perhaps	PERCHANCE
perjured	MAINSWORN
perplexed	NONPLUSSED
perplexed	VAINGLORIOUS
pertinent	APPOSITE
philosophical	METAPHYSICAL
physical	SOMATIC
piece	DETRITUS
pierced	FENESTRATED
pigeon	CUSHAT
piggish	PORCINE
pile	TAAS
piles	CONGERIES
pillar	STANCHION
pinnacle	SERAC
pipe	CALUMET
pirate	CORSAIR
pity	PATHOS
plain	ESPLANADE
plead	OBSECRATE
plead	SUPPLICATE
pleasant	FELICITOUS
pleasantness	AMENITY
pleasurable	HEDONISTIC
pleasure	DELECTATION
pledge	HYPOTHECATE
pledge	RECOGNIZANCE
plot	MACHINATION
plow	EXARATE

plunder	PREDE
plunder	REIVE
poem	ELEGY
poet	POETASTER
pointed	ACULEATE
pointed	APICULATE
pointed	SUBULATED
poison	VENENATE
poisonous	MEPHITIC
poisonous	MIASMIC
polished	LEGGIADROUS
polished	LEVIGATED
ponder	RUMINATE
poor	PENURY
porous	PERMEABLE
postpone	PROROGUE
postponement	CUNCTATION
pouring	AFFUSION
powderize	LEVIGATE
powerless	INERT
powerless	NUGATORY
practical	BANAUSIC
praise	ENCOMIUM
praise	PAEAN
praised	FETED
praising	PLAUSIVE
prayer	DEESIS
prayer	ORISON
precipitating	PLUVIOUS
predict	PRESAGE
prediction	VATICINATION

predictor	PROPHESIER
prehistoric	DOLMEN
prejudice	PREPOSSESSION
preliminary	PREFACTORY
pretender	PANJANDRUM
pretense	SIMULACRUM
pretty	INCONY
prevent	OBVIATE
preventative	PROPHYLACTIC
pride	HUBRIS
priestly	HIERATIC
priestly	SACERDOTAL
primitive	TROGLODYTIC
probe	SPECILLUM
proclaim	ASSEVERATE
proclaim	CONSUBSTANTIATE
proclaim	PROMULGE
proclaiming	INTERNUNCIAL
procrastinating	CUNCTATIVE
procure	EDUCE
productive	GONIMIUM
profane	RIBALD
profit	SUPERLUCRATION
profound	PROFUNDITY
prognostication	HARIOLATION
projection	SCARCEMENT
prone	COUCHANT
prone	RECUMBENT
prophecy	AUGURY
prophetic	FATIDIC
prophetic	SIBYLLINE

prostitute	COURTESAN
prostitute	HETAERA
prostitute	QUEAN
prostitutes	DEMIMONDE
proud	ORGULOUS
proven	DEICTIC
proving	PROBATIVE
proximity	PROPINQUITY
pun	EQUIVOQUE
pun	PARONOMASIA
punctual	PUNCTILIOUS
punish	FUSTIGATE
punishment	SHENDSHIP
purging	LAPACTIC
purplish	HELIOTROPE
pus-like	PURULENT
puzzling	CRYPTIC

q

quadrant	QUARTERN
quarrel	RUCTION
quarrelsome	FRACTIOUS
quarrelsome	PUGNACIOUS
quarrelsome	TRUCULENT
quarters	CANTONMENT
questions	INTERROGATORIES
quibble	CAVIL
quibble	PETTIFOG
quickening	ACCELERANDO

r

racism	ETHNOCENTRICITY
rainy	PLUVIAL
rale	RHONCHUS
rambling	DISCURSIVE
random	ALEATORY
random	DESULTORY
random	STOCHASTIC
ranked	BREVETTED
rape	CONSTUPRATE
rapid heartbeat	TACHYCARDIA
rapture	NYMPHOLEPSY
rascal	SKELLUM
rash	IMPOLITIC
rational	CASUISTIC
ravenous	RAPACIOUS
ravishing	DEFLORATION
reasoning	SYLLOGISM
rebel	INSURGENT
rebirth	PALINGENETIC
rebirth	RENAISSANCE
reception	LEVEE
reckless	TEMERARIOUS

recluse	SOLITUDINARIAN
recoil	RESILE
recoiling	RECUILEMENT
record	PROCÈS-VERBAL
recovery	REPLEVY
recurrence	LEITMOTIF
reddish	GRENADINE
reddish	RUFESCENT
reddish	RUFUS
reduction	DETUMESCENCE
redundancy	NIMIETY
reflecting	RELUCENT
refusing	INACQUIESCENT
regular	METRONOMIC
relaxing	EMOLLIENT
release	REMIT
relentless	INEXORABLE
remembering	ANAMNESIS
remorse	COMPUNCTION
removal	ABSCISSION
removal	EXTIRPATION
removal	RESECTION
remove	ABLATE
renounce	ABJURE
renounce	FORSWEAR
renovate	REDINTEGRATE
repayment	REPARATION
repeat	INGEMINATE
repeated	RECIDIVISM
repetition	ITERATION
repetitious	TAUTOLOGICAL

reporting	REPORTAGE
resemblance	CONSIMILITUDE
resentment	DUDGEON
reserved	DIFFIDENT
residue	RESIDUUM
resistant	RENITENT
respect	OBEISANCE
restoration	APOCATASTASIS
restoration	REVIVIFICATION
restore	REVIVIFY
return	RECRUDESCENCE
return	REPAIR
reveal	EXPOSE
revel	ROISTER
revelation	DENOUEMENT
revenge	ULTION
revile	VILIPEND
revision	RECENSION
revolution	CIRCUMVOLUTION
revolution	JUNTO
revolution	LABEFACTION
riddle	CONUNDRUM
riddle	ENIGMATOGRAPHY
right-handed	DEXTRAL
ringing	TINTINNABULATION
ring-shaped	ANNULAR
riotous	OCHLOCRATIC
rip	DISCERP
risen	ANASTATIC
rising	ANABATIC
rising	ASSURGENT

robber	PICAROON
robber	YEGG
robe	VESTMENT
robot	AUTOMATON
rodlike	BACULINE
rolling	ADVOLUTION
roomy	CAPACIOUS
roomy	COMMODIOUS
rotten	CARIOUS
rough	SCABROUS
roughness	ASPERITY
rubbing	EFFLEURAGE
ruddy	RUTILANT
rude	INSOLENT
ruffian	TATTERDEMALION
rule	MASTERDOM
rural	CAMPESTRAL
rustic	AGRESTIC
rustic	BUCOLIC

S

sacrifice	IMMOLATE
sailboat	BRIGANTINE
saint	ICON
salary	EMOLUMENT
salivation	PTYALOGOGUE
same	IDENTIC
sameness	ANALOGUE
sandy	ARENOSE
sandy	SABULOUS
sarcasm	MORDANCY
sarcastic	SARDONIC
satire	PASQUINADE
satisfy	ASSUAGE
satisfy	SATIATE
saving	SALVIFIC
saying	APOTHEGM
saying	EPIGRAM
scale	ESCALADE
scholar	POLYHISTOR
scholarship	ERUDITION
scoundrel	PICARESQUE
scoundrel	ROGUE

screen	ICONOSTASIS
seal	CACHET
seam	RAPHE
search	INDAGATE
seasickness	NAUPATHIA
seasonable	TEMPESTIVE
seductress	FEMME FATALE
seize	ARROGATE
seize	RAVISH
self-arousal	AUTOEROTISM
self-assertive	BUMPTIOUS
self-deprivation	MASOCHISM
self-taught	AUTODIDACTIC
senile	ANILE
senior	DOYEN
seniorhood	SENECTITUDE
sensitive	SENSIFEROUS
sensual	VOLUPTUARY
sentimental	MAWKISH
sentimentality	BATHOS
separate	DISCRETE
separate	PRESCIND
separate	SEVERAL
separation	SEQUESTRATION
serial	POLYSTICHOUS
sermon	HOMILY
servant	FACTOTUM
servitude	THRALLDOM
servitude	VASSALAGE
sever	SUNDER

sexual	AMATORY
sexual	APHRODISIAC
sexual	CONCUPISCENT
sexuality	CONCUPISCENCE
shady	UMBRAGEOUS
shaking	JECTIGATION
shameful	INGLORIOUS
shapeless	AMORPHOUS
shaven	UNBARBED
shavings	EXCELSIOR
sheathed	VAGINATE
sheltered	ENSCONCED
shield	ESCUTCHEON
shifty	LOUCHE
ship	XEBEC
shipwreck	NAUFRAGE
shoeless	DISCALCED
shore	LITTORAL
short-lived	EPHEMERAL
showy	PEDANTIC
shrew	VIRAGO
shrew	XANTHIPPE
sieve	ECTETHMOID
sigh	SUSPIRATION
sightless	TYPHLOSIS
silent	TACITURN
silver	ARGENT
sinful	PIACULAR
single	MONOGRAPHIC
sisterly	SORORAL

sixtieth	SEXAGESIMAL
skeptical	NIHILISTIC
skillful	DAEDAL
skullcap	ZUCCHETTO
skunk	CONEPATE
slander	ANIMADVERSION
slander	ASPERSION
slander	CALUMNY
slander	TRADUCE
slanderous	MALEDICENT
slang	ARGOT
slavery	THRALL
slavish	OBSEQUIOUS
sleepwalker	NOCTAMBULIST
sleepwalking	SOMNAMBULISM
sleepy	HYPNAGOGIC
sleepy	SOMNOLENT
sleepy	SOPORIFIC
slender	ECTOMORPHIC
slimy	MUCILAGIOUS
slogan	SHIBBOLETH
sluggish	TORPID
sluggishness	LANGUOR
sluglike	LIMACINE
small	LILLIPUTIAN
smelling	OSMATIC
smooth	GLABROUS
smooth	PROFLUENT
smoothly	MELLIFLUOUS
smug	PRIGGISH

snake	OPHIDIAN
snowy	NIVEOUS
soak	MACERATE
socialism	ETATISM
society	SODALITY
sodomy	PEDERASTY
soiled	SCROFULOUS
solicit	IMPORTUNATE
soluble	HYDROPHILIC
somber	SOMBROUS
soothing	ABIRRITANT
soothing	DEMULCENT
sophisticated	SOIGNÉ
sound	SONANCE
soundless	ASONANT
soup	BISQUE
sour	ACETOUS
souring	ACESCENT
source	PROVENIENCE
sparkle	CORUSCATE
speaking	ELOCUTION
speckled	PIED
speculate	EXTRAPOLATE
speediness	CELERITY
spherical	GLOBOSE
spicy	PIQUANT
spinning	STROBIC
spiral	HELICAL
spiral	TURBINATION
spirit	ANIMUS

spirit	ÉLAN
sponge	MOREL
sponsorship	AEGIS
spotted	LENTIGINOUS
spotted	LITURATE
spotted	PIEBALD
spread	METASTASIZE
spreading	PROPAGATION
spreading	PROTUBERANT
spring	VERNAL
sprinkle	BESPANGLE
stab	SPEET
stabbing	LANCINATING
stagger	WAMBLE
staggering	TITUBATION
stake	PALISADE
stalking	PREDACEOUS
stammer	BALBUTIATE
standard	NORMATIVE
starchy	FARINACEOUS
starry	SIDEREAL
steady	EQUABLE
steal	FILCH
steal	PURLOINED
steal	SPOLIATE
stealthily	FURTIVELY
steep	PRECIPITOUS
steeple	FLECHE
stench	MEPHITIS
sterilization	ASEXUALIZATION

sterilize	AUTOCLAVE
stern	AUSTERE
stern	DOUR
stew	SLUMGULLION
sticky	VISCID
stimulation	ERETHISM
sting	ACULEUS
sting	TEREBRATE
stingy	PENURIOUS
stinking	FETID
stinking	MALODOROUS
stop	BELAY
stop	KIBOSH
storage	CACHE
storyteller	RACONTEUR
straight	GEODESIC
strip	DENUDE
stripping	NUDATION
strong	PUISSANT
stronghold	FASTNESS
stubborn	MULISH
stubborn	RECALCITRANT
stubborn	REFRACTORY
studio	ATELIER
study	LUCUBRATION
stupid	DOLTISH
stupid	GORMLESS
stupid	MORONIC
stupidity	STUPEFACTION
stupid person	BOEOTIAN

stuttering	PSELLISM
submissive	UXORIOUS
subordinate	SUBALTERN
subtlety	QUODLIBET
suffocation	HYPOXEMIA
sugar	XYLOSE
suitable	BESEEM
suitable	IDONEOUS
suitcase	IMPEDIMENTA
suitcase	PORTMANTEAU
summary	COMPENDIUM
sun-centered	HELIOCENTRIC
sunstroke	HELIOSIS
superficial	DILETTANTE
superficial	SCIOLISTIC
supernatural	PRETERNATURAL
supplement	CODICIL
supplier	PURVEYOR
supportive	JANISSARY
supreme	SOVEREIGN
surliness	CHUFFINESS
surname	COGNOMEN
surname	PATRONYMIC
surplus	SURPLUSAGE
surround	ENCINCTURE
surrounding	AMBIENT
surrounding	CIRCUMJACENT
swagger	HECTOR
swallowing	DEGLUTITION
swear	ADJURE
sweetheart	DOWSABEL

swelling	GIBBOUS
swelling	TUBER
swindler	GRIFTER
swishing	FROUFROU
swollen	CHILBLAINED
swollen	TUMESCENT
symbol	EXPONENT
symbol	IDEOGRAM
systematist	TAXONOMIST

tact	SAVOIR FAIRE
tactless	GAUCHE
tailless	ANUROUS
tailored	SARTORIAL
talkative	EXPATIATING
talkative	GARRULOUS
talkative	LOQUACIOUS
talkativeness	GARRULITY
tangent	ASYMPTOTE
tangible	TACTILE
tapering	LANCEOLATE
tasteful	PRECIOSITY
tasteless	INSIPID
teaching	DIDACTIC
teaching	HEURISTIC
teaching	PEDAGOGY
tearful	LACHRYMOSE
tearing	AVULSION
teasing	BADINAGE
temperament	PANTAGRUELISM
temporarily	PROVISORILY
tenacious	PERTINACIOUS

tent	YURT
terminate	DISESTABLISH
terminate	SURCEASE
terrestrial	SUBLUNARY
thawing	EUTECTIC
theatrical	DRAMATURGIC
theatrical	HISTRIONIC
theft	PRIGGERY
theory	HYPOTHESIS
thickened	INSPISSATED
thickened	PACHYDERMATOUS
thicket	BOSCAGE
thicket	CHAPARRAL
thin	GRACILE
third	TERTIARY
thirst	POLYDIPSIA
thrash	YERK
thread	CAPILLAMENT
thrice-married	TRIGAMOUS
thrill	FRISSON
throng	UMBERMENT
throw	JACULATE
throwback	ATAVISM
throw out	DEFENESTRATE
thrusting	ERUMPENT
tilt	CANT
timetable	SYNCHRONISM
timid	TIMOROUS
tingling	PARESTHESIA
tiny	DIMINUTIVE
tireless	INDEFATIGABLE

title	RUBRIC
toast	WASSAIL
tomboy	HOYDEN
tongue	LANGUET
tongue-tied	ELINGUID
toothache	ODONTALGIA
tracker	ICHNEYMON
traitor	QUISLING
transcription	AMANUENSIS
transform	TRANSMOGRIFY
transform	TRANSMUTE
translation	RELEXIFICATION
transparent	DIAPHANOUS
transparent	HYALOD
transparent	PELLUCID
trap	ENTOIL
treelike	DENDROPHILOUS
trembling	TREMULOUS
triangular	SAGITTATE
trick	ARTIFICE
trick	WAGGERY
trickery	LEGERDEMAIN
trifecta	TRIPLICITY
trifle	BAGATELLE
trifle	FIDDLE-FADDLE
trinity	HYPOSTASAS
trio	TROIKA
trivial	DOGGEREL
troublemaker	FOMENTER
true	AXIOMATIC
trustworthy	MORIGERATE

truth	VERISIMILITUDE
truthful	VERIDICAL
tubular	CANNULAR
tumor	NEOPLASM
turncoat	RECREANT
turreted	CASTELLATED
twilight	GLOAMING
typical	QUINTESSENTIAL

U

unauthorized	ULTRA VIRES
unbeliever	INFIDEL
unbiased	INDIFFERENT
uncertain	IDIOPATHIC
uncertainty	DUBIOSITY
unchangeable	IMMUTABLE
unchronological	ANACHRONISTIC
unclear	AMPHIGORY
uncle-like	AVUNCULAR
uncompromising	INTRANSIGENT
unconsciousness	NARCOSIS
uncultured	ILLIBERAL
understanding	INTUITED
understanding	PERSPICACIOUS
understatement	LITOTES
understatement	MEIOSIS
unedited	UNEXPURGATED
uneducated	BOOBOISIE
unfinished	QUAB
unflappability	IMPERTURBATION
unfriendly	INIMICAL

ungrammatical	SOLECISTIC
unilateral	SECUND
unintelligibility	GLOSSOLALIA
union	ANASTOMOSIS
unique	SINGULAR
unique	SUI GENERIS
united	SOLIDARY
unload	DISGORGE
unmixable	IMMISCIBLE
unnecessary	SUPEREROGATORY
unnecessary	SUPERFLUOUS
unorthodox	HETERODOX
unprepared	IMPROVIDENT
unreasonableness	CHAUVINISM
unreturned	UNREQUITED
unruliness	OBSTREPEROUSNESS
unruly	ACERBIC
unruly	RESTIVE
unsalable	INALIENABLE
unsatisfying	JEJUNE
unsolvable	IRREMEDIABLE
unspeakable	INEFFABLE
unstable	LABILE
unusual	RECHERCHÉ
unusual	SELCOUTH
unusualness	DEUTEROPATHY
unwise	ANSERINE
upkeep	SUSTENTATION
uproot	DERACINATE
urbane	SVELTE

urbanization	CONURBATION
urgency	EXIGENCY
urgent	NECESSITOUS
urination	MICTURITION
usefulness	UTILITARIANISM

V

vagrant	CAIRD
vagrant	CLOCHARD
vagrant	VAGROM
valor	VALIANCE
valve	PETCOCK
vanish	EVANESCE
vanity	NARCISSISM
vengeance	COMMINATION
vent	FUMAROLE
ventilate	AERATE
ventilate	INSUFFLATE
verbiage	PERIPHRASIS
verifiable	EMPIRICAL
veritable	EXISTENTIAL
vestibule	NARTHEX
villain	MISCREANT
visions	PHANTASMAGORIA
volcanic	IGNEOUS
vomit-inducing	EMETIC
vomiting	HYPEREMESIS
V-shaped	CHEVRON
vulgarity	BILLINGSGATE

Somerset County Library System of NJ
Mary Jacobs branch

Checkouts for KOLL LAK

1,000 most challenging words /
428.1 SCH
33665000801432
Due Date: 1/26/2018

Twilight /
MEYER
33665024395387
Due Date: 1/26/2018

The siren /
CASS
33665029555712
Due Date: 1/26/2018

Word for word /
423.12 SNY
33665022400452
Due Date: 1/26/2018

**You saved $68.88 today by using your
library card!**

To renew your materials, Visit us online at
SCLSNJ.org.

1/5/2018 3:27:47 PM

W

wager	IMPONE
wail	ULULATE
walk	PEREGRINATE
wall	PARAPET
wander	DIVAGATE
wander	GALLIVANT
wander	MAUNDER
wandering	EVAGATION
wandering	SKIMBLE-SKAMBLE
warning	CAVEAT
warning	PREMONITORY
warrant	CAPIAS
wart	EXCRESCENCE
wart	THYMION
wash	DETERGE
washing	ABLUTION
waste	DROSS
waste	OFFAL
wasteful	ORDURE
waterfall	SAULT
wavy	GYROSE
weak	ADYNAMIC

weak	ASTHENIC
weak	THEWLESS
weaken	ATTENUATE
weaken	EMASCULATE
weaken	LABEFY
wealthy	SYBARITE
weaning	ABLACTATION
web-footed	TOTIPALMATE
weekly	HEBDOMEDAL
weird	ELDRITCH
well-dressed	CONCINNOUS
western	OCCIDENTAL
wetness	HUMECTANT
whim	CROTCHET
whine	PULE
whine	YAMMER
whip	FLAGELLATE
whirling	VERTIGINOUS
whirlpool	MAELSTROM
whisper	SUSURRATION
whispering	SUSURROUS
white	ALBESCENT
white	LEUKOUS
whiten	ETIOLATE
whitening	ALBICATION
wicked	FACINOROUS
wicked	FLAGITIOUS
wicked	INIQUITOUS
widowhood	VIDUITY
wig	PERUKE
wild	ROYTISH

wildness	FERITY
winding	ANFRACTUOUS
winding	LABYRINTHIAN
winding	SINUOUS
winegrower	VIGNERON
wine study	OENOLOGY
wisdom	SAGACITY
wisdom	SAPIENCE
wish	VELLEITY
wishful	DESIDERATE
womanhood	MULIEBRITY
wooded	ARBOREOUS
wooded	BUSKY
woody	XYLOID
word	PALABRA
wordiness	CIRCUMLOCUTION
wordy	PERIPHRASTIC
wordy	PROLIX
wordy	SESQUIPEDALIAN
worker	ROUSTABOUT
worried	SOLICITOUS
worsening	INGRAVESCENT
worthless	DRAFFISH
worthless	FECKLESS
wrinkled	RUGOSE
writer	SCRIVENER

X

xed	DISESTABLISHED
X-ray	ROENTGEN

y

yahoo	PHILISTINE
yawn	OSCITATION
yearly	ETESIAN
yearning	REPINE
yellow	XANTHIC
yielding	EMULSIVE
youth	VIRIDITY
youthful	JUVENESCENT

Z

zealous	FERVID
zealous	PERFERVID
zoned	CIRCUMSCRIBED